CONTENTS

KT-559-640

Shop online at Waterstones.com

2 Introduction

3 Books for 0–3 year-olds
– Very First Books
– First Books
– First Skills

10 Favourite Characters

14 Reading Aloud to Kids

16 Books for 3–5 year-olds
– Nursery Rhymes
– Picture Books

27 Books for 5–8 year-olds
– Learning to Read
– Developing Readers
– Audio
– Confident Readers

44 Fairytales and Myths

45 Poetry

46 Classics and Gifts

48 Books for 9–12 year-olds
– Reluctant Readers

71 Books for Teens
– First Adult

86 Non-Fiction

87 Activities

89 Hobbies

91 Reference
– Encyclopedias
and Dictionaries
– Languages
and Atlases
– Our Planet
– Nature
– Science and the Body
– History
– Religion

102 Study Guides

112 Dyslexia

114 Books That Can Help

120 Indexes

CONTENTS

WELCOME to the
Waterstone's Guide to Kids' Books

Children's books have gone through a real renaissance in recent years. The range, quality and innovation available today is astounding; from touchy-feely books for babies through interactive encyclopedias and compelling magical stories that everyone seems to be reading. With so much available in every genre, choosing the right books for the children in your life can be difficult.

Drawing on the expertise and passion of our children's booksellers, we've produced this guide to help you discover the best new books available for children. It's packed with hundreds of recommendations for our favourite books, fact and fiction, and we've included basic information on common queries; what to look for when choosing stories or educational resources; how to help reluctant readers get into books; tips on reading aloud to young kids, and a comprehensive subject index.

This guide is divided by age group just like our kids' areas in store. Each section has a short introduction with the books grouped by their theme, content or style to give you the perfect starting point.

We hope you'll find this guide a useful introduction to the world of Waterstone's kids' books. At your local store you'll find bright, colourful kids' sections, regular events, and, most importantly, knowledgeable, dedicated children's booksellers who love reading and are very happy to help you and your child discover even more great books, so please just ask! If you can't get to a store, just visit Waterstones.com, which offers almost everything you'd find in one of our shops – you can even 'Ask a Bookseller' for advice.

Happy reading!

THE WATERSTONE'S CHILDREN'S TEAM

Key: (�noise) Also available as an audiobook
      (RR) Particularly suitable for reluctant readers

BOOKS FOR 0-3 YEAR-OLDS

It is never too early to introduce your child to books. There are lots of gorgeous books available for the very young, designed to help stimulate and educate your baby and be fun for both parent and child.

Things to look for when choosing books for a baby are big pictures, bright colours, simple design and strongly defined shapes. Look for illustrations that a baby will recognise from everyday life, for instance, people, toys, food or bathtime.

Many baby books incorporate a variety of innovative novelty features that develop and encourage the different senses. Help your baby to participate with you in lifting the flap, looking through the peephole, pressing buttons to hear sounds, or running fingers over different textures – from silky smooth to scratchy and rough. As your child grows older and more confident in their dexterity move on to more complex board books to increase familiarity with books.

Please turn the page for a selection of our tried and tested favourites.

Free delivery to store at Waterstones.com

VERY FIRST BOOKS...

Baby's First Cot Book

by Fiona Watt and Stella Baggott

ISBN 9780746087800   RRP £6.99

'This cot book can be used from birth and doubles as a cloth book. With its bright, contrasting patterns and simple illustrations it's a perfect way to stimulate vision and introduce books to your baby.'

Daniella Seaman, Waterstone's Norwich Arcade

Playtime Peekaboo!

ISBN 9781405309226   RRP £4.99

'This simple lift-the-flap format never fails to delight and entertain babies. Play peekaboo together with this fun, colourful book.'

Arlene Crummy, Waterstone's Newry

Clackety Clacks: Bee

by Luana Rinaldo

ISBN 9781405047685   RRP £3.99

'I love these colourful baby books with their easy-to-hold handles – ideal for little hands – and chunky pages that make a satisfying clackety-clack when shaken about.'

Kate Skipper, Waterstone's Children's Team

Snuggletime Series

by Fiona Watt and Catherine MacKinnon

ISBN 9780746063682   RRP £5.99

'These simple stories with cute pictures are the perfect first books. With pictures of familiar things, their touchy-feely, sparkly bits engage baby's interest. Lovely.'

Sarah Williamson, Waterstone's Tunbridge Wells

Rainbow Fun

by Emma Dodd and Mike Jolley

ISBN 9781904513605   RRP £4.99

'Created especially for babies aged 6-18 months, this is a great introduction to colours. Bold illustrations and a simple rhyming text help to stimulate verbal and visual development.'

Kate Skipper, Waterstone's Children's Team

My First Signs

by Annie Kubler

ISBN 9781904550044   RRP £4.99

'One of the best baby signing books around, full of simple, colourful illustrations and helpful tips, it's ideal to share with babies as young as seven months.'

Becky Hunt, Waterstone's Worcester City Arcade

That's Not My... Series

RRP £5.99

'With everything from 'angel' to 'truck', there's sure to be a subject to fascinate your little one from this touchy-feely range. With myriad textures, it's a great concept, and a really lovely presentation.'

Kate Phillips,
Waterstone's Oxford

Old MacDonald: A Hand Puppet Book

ISBN 9780545026031   RRP £6.99

'This is both a brilliantly fun, interactive book that parents and children will enjoy, and a great way to learn new words and practise recognising common animals.'

Manel Awajan,
Waterstone's Lincoln

Buggy Buddies: Farm

by Jo Lodge
ISBN 9780333781203   RRP £3.99

'This small, brightly coloured book is perfect for little children as it helps with visual stimulation, and teaches different textures. Plus you can fasten it to your buggy!'

Carrie Innes,
Waterstone's Aberdeen
Union Bridge

Splish, Splash, Splosh

by Luana Rinaldo
ISBN 9780746077375   RRP £5.99

'This jolly, bold bath book will have babies enthralled both in the bath and out of it. With its soft, durable pages and the squeaky little fish attached, this is a delight.'

Vicky Hutchings,
Waterstone's Cardiff The Hayes

Busy Airport

by Rebecca Finn
ISBN 9781405047951   RRP £4.99

'This colourful book with bits that turn and lift will captivate your child. You can make the planes fly and luggage move round just like a real airport!'

Georgia Stanford,
Waterstone's Worcester
The Shambles

LADYBIRD BOOKS...

6

Ladybird books have been loved by toddlers and trusted by adults for generations. The easy-to-use, clear and colourful books stimulate children to learn and provide enjoyment for the whole family. Ladybird can take you from baby books through early learning to first readers. Here is a selection of our favourites.

First Fairytales Series

RRP £4.99

'Suitable for one to three year-olds, these touchy-feely books are a simple, memorable introduction to fairytales.'

Fiona Nolan,
Waterstone's Dublin Dawson Street

Baby Touch Series

ISBN 9781844225897
Available in various prices and formats

'This series can be used from birth to stimulate baby with the bright colours, tactile pages and elementary words.'

Jenny Lee,
Editor

Minis Series

RRP £1.99

'These stylish little books are a great introduction to reading. Perfect for two to six year-olds.'

Kate Hancock,
Waterstone's Children's Team

Noisy Noisy Series

ISBN 9781846467943   RRP £7.99

'Toddlers will love these innovative sound books, which have a different noise on every page. Plus the battery can be replaced, ensuring endless fun!'

Jo Stanford,
Waterstone's Tunbridge Wells

FIRST BOOKS ...

Farmyard Tales

Available in various prices and formats

'This series is ideal for toddlers, encompassing everything from a wind-up tractor book to a treasury of stories. The illustrations are wonderful, and the text simple, amusing and informative. Don't forget to look out for the little yellow duck on every page.'

Laura Dobbie,
Waterstone's Banbury

My Mummy's Bag
by Paul Hanson
ISBN 9780761148203   RRP £12.99

'Every child likes to explore mummy's bag. This brilliant novelty book allows your little one to do just that, without losing anything vital!'

Laura Sayers,
Waterstone's Merry Hill

My Terrific Tractor Book
ISBN 9781405319133   RRP £9.99

'Fabulously noisy, with lift-the-flap, pop-up and touchy-feely features. This bright, interactive book will delight tractor-loving toddlers, encouraging use of all their senses.'

Amy Fox,
Waterstone's Southend

Little Ballerina Dancing Book
by Fiona Watt
ISBN 9780746077337   RRP £9.99

'This beautiful book for your little ballerina encourages movement to some classic ballet tunes on the included CD. My little girls love it.'

Michelle Lever,
Waterstone's Bournemouth Castle Point

FIRST BOOKS...

Dear Zoo
by Rod Campbell
ISBN 9780230015258   RRP £4.99

'I love this book. There are lift-the-flap surprises and kids will want to chime in with naming the familiar zoo animals behind each door. Great fun.'

Kim Retallack,
Waterstone's Plymouth
New George Street

Janet and Allan Ahlberg

Available in various prices and formats

'These books are pure genius. The words and pictures work together in total harmony, providing entertainment whether it is the first or thousandth time you read the book. These will be firm favourites long past babyhood.'

Sarah Skinner,
Waterstone's Norwich Castle Street

Say Hello to the Animals!
by Ian Whybrow and Tim Warnes
ISBN 9780230528598   RRP £5.99

'Moo, oink and baa your way around a farmyard of animals. With its touchy-feely pages and rhyming story, every toddler will want to read this again and again.'

Natalie Likness,
Waterstone's Staines

Goodnight Moon
by Margaret Wise Brown
ISBN 9780333961070   RRP £4.99

'This classic book has been making children smile for over 60 years. Beautiful words coupled with simple illustrations make it a perfect early book for any young child.'

Jo Stanford,
Waterstone's Tunbridge Wells

Calm Down Boris!
by Sam Lloyd
ISBN 9781840114478   RRP £8.99

'Part book, part hand puppet, this wacky book will keep you and you child giggling for hours. It's a great, fun way of interacting through books.'

Jo Stanford,
Waterstone's Tunbridge Wells

FIRST SKILLS ...

First Picture ABC

by Felicity Brooks

ISBN 9780746062708   RRP £8.99

'Full of visually exciting, colourful illustrations, this is a wonderful 'first letters' book that children can look at over and over again. The padded cover and sturdy pages ensure it will hold up to repeated use.'

Emma Cresswell,
Waterstone's Crewe

Ten Wriggly Wiggly Caterpillars

by Debbie Tarbett

ISBN 9781845060275   RRP £7.99

'This is a fantastic interactive counting book with tiny 3D caterpillars and a butterfly surprise at the end. It will keep children entertained as they practise their numbers.'

Izzy Kertland,
Waterstone's Manchester Arndale

Usborne First Experiences Series

ISBN 9780746066607   RRP £3.99

'Fun, friendly and informative, these gentle stories give children an idea of what to expect, whether they are starting school or having a new brother or sister.'

Lisa Hunt,
Waterstone's Milton Keynes
Silbury Avenue

Catch That Goat!

by Polly Alakija

ISBN 9781846860560   RRP £5.99

'In this hide-and-seek counting book, bright illustrations show how busy the market is as Ayoka hunts for her goat. See how much trouble it has caused!'

Andrea Don,
Waterstone's Canterbury Rose Lane

First Colours

by Felicity Brooks and Jo Litchfield

ISBN 9780746073339   RRP £8.99

'This gorgeous board book is designed to introduce very young children to colours. The sturdy pages are great for little hands to explore.'

Hannah Liddell,
Waterstone's Redditch

Topsy and Tim Series

by Jean and Gareth Adamson

ISBN 9781904351252   RRP £2.50

'The lovable characters Topsy and Tim are wonderful companions for children through some early experiences. They do everything, from going camping to having nits!'

Hattie Bavin,
Waterstone's Gloucester

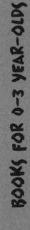

FAVOURITE CHARACTERS...

Young children form lasting friendships with favourite characters like 'Thomas the Tank Engine' or 'Charlie and Lola', and they are a great way to introduce kids to books, and hold their interest as they learn to read. From books for babies to older storybooks, a favourite character can accompany a child from their first book through to independent reading.

Character books appear in a wide variety of innovative, engaging formats: there are activity books, books that make noises, have surprise endings or even some that have wheels! Many of these characters go through the same life experiences as a child, so Spot starts school, Lola refuses to eat tomatoes and Thomas learns to count. Look out for the 'little libraries' format, bite-sized books ideal for car journeys or party bags.

In the Night Garden
TM & © Ragdoll
Worldwide Limited 2007.

In the Night Garden

Available in various prices and formats

'Kids adore Makka Pakka and friends. A perfect series for entertaining toddlers as they love the funny words and names.'

Shelley George,
Waterstone's Southampton Above Bar

Ragdoll

Kipper

by Mick Inkpen   Available in various prices and formats

'Everyone has a soft spot for waggly-tailed Kipper. This cute pup loves having adventures with his friends, making these books brilliant to share and read aloud.'

Emma Wearn,
Waterstone's Southampton Above Bar

Illustrations © Mick Inkpen

Spot

by Eric Hill   **Available in various prices and formats**

'The simple stories and lift-the-flap illustrations make Spot books fun and interactive. This loveable little dog should be part of every child's introduction to reading.'

Jo Stanford,
Waterstone's Tunbridge Wells

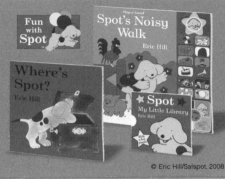

© Eric Hill/Salspot, 2008

Thomas the Tank Engine

Available in various prices and formats

'It's been over 60 years since we first met Thomas the little blue engine and his friends, and the gang still thrill today. All the trains' easily identifiable characteristics make them perfect for introducing ideas about emotions and friendship.'

Davey Shields,
Waterstone's University of East Anglia

Thomas the Tank Engine & Friends TM Based on the Railway Series by the Reverend W Awdry. © 2008 Gullane (Thomas) LLC. A HIT Entertainment company. Thomas the Tank Engine & Friends and Thomas & Friends are trademarks of Gullane (Thomas) Limited. Thomas the Tank Engine & Friends & Design is Reg. U.S. Pat. & Tm. Off.

Disney

Available in various prices and formats

'These novelisations and activity books based on classic Disney movies are a great way to introduce books to children. You too can roar with Simba, or dazzle like Ariel!'

Jenny Lee,
Editor

FAVOURITE CHARACTERS...

Charlie and Lola

by Lauren Child   Available in various prices and formats

'Kids are undoubtedly funny, and that's perfectly captured in Lauren Child's brilliant brother and sister duo. Quirky illustrations and hilarious stories – real giggle-your-socks-off stuff!'

Sarah Williamson,
Waterstone's Tunbridge Wells

Charlie and Lola copyright ©
Tiger Aspect Productions Ltd/
Lauren Child 2008

Dr. Seuss Properties tm &
© 1957 Dr. Seuss Enterprises,
L.P. All Rights Reserved

Dr. Seuss

Available in various prices and formats

'Dr. Seuss stories are full of wacky characters and brilliant pictures. The repetitiveness of the silly rhymes makes these ideal for practising reading.'

Kirstin McCarle,
Waterstone's St. Andrews

Winnie-the-Pooh

by A.A. Milne   Available in various prices and formats

'For over 80 years, the bear of 'very little brain' and his motley crew of co-dwellers have been charming and amusing readers of all ages. There is something for everyone in the world of the Hundred Acre Wood.'

Helen Johnson,
Waterstone's University of East Anglia

Text © A. A. Milne and line
illustrations © E. H. Shepard.

FAVOURITE CHARACTERS

W kids' books

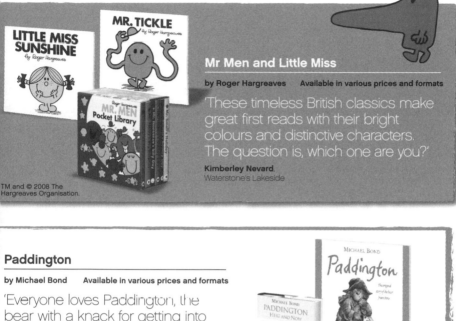

Mr Men and Little Miss

by Roger Hargreaves   Available in various prices and formats

'These timeless British classics make great first reads with their bright colours and distinctive characters. The question is, which one are you?'

Kimberley Nevard,
Waterstone's Lakeside

TM and © 2008 The Hargreaves Organisation.

Paddington

by Michael Bond   Available in various prices and formats

'Everyone loves Paddington, the bear with a knack for getting into trouble. Available as picture books, activity books and short story collections, they are the perfect books to grow up with.'

Daniella Seaman,
Waterstone's Norwich Arcade

Peter Rabbit

by Beatrix Potter   Available in various prices and formats

'Beatrix Potter is famous for her timeless series of little books about animals from the English countryside. The white covers and delicate watercolours make them perfect gifts for readers of all ages'.

Kirstin McCarle,
Waterstone's St. Andrews

© F. Warne & Co., 2008

FAVOURITE CHARACTERS

READING ALOUD TO KIDS...

Reading aloud to your child is one of the most rewarding things you can do together. Children love the warmth and intimacy of a reading session with a favourite adult. Reading aloud with a child develops their listening and talking skills as well as reading ability. It may seem daunting to do at first, but with a few tips and practice you'll soon find it easy.

Don't stop reading aloud with your child when they have learnt to read, you can still enjoy more complex books together that they wouldn't be able to tackle on their own — you'll soon be having animated discussions predicting plot twists and what will happen next.

Our tips for reading aloud:

- Read the book through to yourself first taking note of the rhythms

- Pronounce each separate word distinctively

- Try using different voices for each character

- Follow the story in the pictures — ask your child to explain what is happening

- Encourage your child to interact, for example turning the pages or following the words with their finger

- Encourage your child to chant along with familiar phrases

- Relax and have fun

Kids love the comfort of the familiar, so be prepared to read the same book over and over again!

NURSERY RHYMES...

Nursery rhymes can play an important part in the learning to read process as they help reinforce vocabulary and sentence structures in a fun and memorable way.

Nursery Rhymes

by Debi Gliori
ISBN 9781405320153   RRP £7.99

'Lovingly illustrated, with plenty of sing-along potential, young children will fall in love with this nursery rhyme and CD collection. It's bound to bring a smile to their face.'

Kimberley Nevard,
Waterstone's Lakeside

My Favourite Nursery Rhymes

by Tony Ross
ISBN 9781842707463   RRP £8.99

'A lovely collection of classic nursery rhymes by the award-winning Tony Ross. Both witty and nostalgic, with charming illustrations, this is a perfect gift book to read aloud together.'

Becky Jarvis,
Waterstone's High Wycombe

Playtime Rhymes

by Sally Gardner
ISBN 9780752860886   RRP £9.99

'This sumptuous book of favourite playground action rhymes is a great mix of the contemporary and traditional. It comes with 50 minutes of fun on CD. Absolutely brilliant!'

Sue Allen,
Waterstone's Merry Hill

Michael Foreman's Nursery Rhymes

by Michael Foreman
ISBN 9780744598209   RRP £9.99

'All the best-loved rhymes are here in this comprehensive gem of a book. I love how the fabulous, colourful pictures link one rhyme to the next.'

Carol Dixon-Smith,
Waterstone's Windsor

NURSERY RHYMES

BOOKS FOR 3-5 YEAR-OLDS

PICTURE BOOKS

From cosy bedtime reads to rowdy read-a-longs, picture books are the gateway to the magic of reading. They help children develop verbal dexterity, vocabulary and imagination. Kids at this stage love being able to recognise words for themselves that they see in books or in everyday life.

The picture books most likely to appeal to your child combine engaging illustrations with a great narrative, and a punchy ending. There are many great picture books to choose from, so consider books with themes that suit your child's tastes and interests.

Younger kids love funny stories – anything involving pants is guaranteed to raise a giggle – while children of all ages respond to stories with jaunty refrains or noises that they can join in with; millions of families across the land have chanted together "Oh help! Oh no! It's a gruffalo!" (see page 19).

To help you choose the right book for your child we have divided our selection into younger, simpler books, and older ones that have a bit more complexity. Our booksellers will also be happy to give you further advice and recommendations.

PICTURE BOOKS FOR THE VERY YOUNG...

The Very Hungry Caterpillar

by Eric Carle
ISBN 9780140569322   RRP £6.99

'Everyone loves this hungry caterpillar! One of my favourites as a child; fun, informative and superbly illustrated in Carle's unique collage style, it's a must-have classic.'

Sarah Williamson,
Waterstone's Tunbridge Wells

Meg and Mog

by Helen Nicoll and Jan Pieńkowski
ISBN 9780141501505   RRP £5.99

'This timeless book has bright, bold illustrations and simple, effective text that youngsters will adore. Immensely enjoyable, and a personal favourite of mine.'

Amy Fox,
Waterstone's Southend

Rosie's Walk

by Pat Hutchins
ISBN 9780099413998   RRP £5.99

'Don't be deceived by the simplicity of this story. With the clumsy fox, and rich illustrations, there is plenty for toddlers to look at and talk about. Look out for its surprise ending.'

Hattie Bavin,
Waterstone's Gloucester

Handa's Surprise

by Eileen Browne
ISBN 9780744536348   RRP £5.99

'This lovely African tale teaches the names of fruits, animals and colours, as well as having glorious, vivid pictures and a brilliant twist at the end.'

Lisa Hunt,
Waterstone's Milton Keynes
Midsummer Arcade

Guess How Much I Love You

by Sam McBratney and Anita Jeram
ISBN 9781406300406   RRP £5.99

'Big Nutbrown Hare and Little Nutbrown Hare try to explain just how much they mean to each other in this warm and gentle story. Perfect, snuggly bedtime reading.'

Emma Wearn,
Waterstone's Southampton
Above Bar

Dig Dig Digging

by Margaret Mayo and Alex Ayliffe
ISBN 9781841210803   RRP £5.99

'My two year-old nephew loves vehicles and has demanded that I read this alliterated book to him again and again. It won't be long until I know it off by heart!'

Manel Awajan,
Waterstone's Lincoln

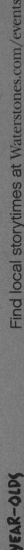

YOUNGER PICTURE BOOKS...

Lost and Found

by Oliver Jeffers
ISBN 9780007150366   RRP £5.99

'I just love Oliver Jeffers' picture books. This beautifully illustrated tale of the friendship between a lonely boy and a penguin is ideal for reading together.'

Sarah Williamson,
Waterstone's Tunbridge Wells

Where the Wild Things Are

by Maurice Sendak
ISBN 9780099408390   RRP £5.99

'This is a great book telling the story of mischief-maker Max and his night-time adventure meeting and taming the Wild Things. A fantastic classic with unforgettable pictures.'

Tam Malkiewicz,
Waterstone's Stirling

Who's In the Loo?

by Jeanne Willis and Adrian Reynolds
ISBN 9781842706985   RRP £5.9

'This has to be one of my favourite picture books. Children of all ages will love this 'naughty' story and its bright, boisterous illustrations.'

Katie Waters,
Waterstone's Edinburgh West End

Not Now, Bernard

by David McKee
ISBN 9780099240501   RRP £4.99

'Monsters are loose in Bernard's house but his parents are too preoccupied to notice! A much-loved classic my parents were forced to read to me again and again.'

John Lloyd,
Waterstone's Bath

Mister Magnolia

by Quentin Blake
ISBN 9780099400424   RRP £5.99

'Mister Magnolia has many wonderful things – friends, family, mice and owls. However, he only has one boot... I love this romping, rhyming story – great for reading aloud.'

Davey Shields,
Waterstone's University of East Anglia

Penguin

by Polly Dunbar
ISBN 9781406312461   RRP £5.99

'This is one of my favourite picture books; the bold, simple illustrations complement the story of a burgeoning friendship wonderfully, making it a joy to share together.'

Izzy Kertland,
Waterstone's Manchester Arndale

JULIA DONALDSON AND AXEL SCHEFFLER

What do you get when you combine writer Julia Donaldson and illustrator Axel Scheffler? Picture book magic!

Donaldson writes in the most beautiful bouncing rhythm that's a dream to read aloud. There is just the right level of repetition in her prose, and she pulls off the difficult trick of producing stories that entertain both the adult reader and their younger audience.

And not forgetting the other half of the super duo – Axel Scheffler. His illustrations are wonderfully expressive, full of bright colours and precise, neat details. They have a timeless quality that works brilliantly to enhance and energise Julia's words.

The pair are best known for the undisputed classic 'The Gruffalo', with its tale of brains defeating brawn, but try also the magical story of 'The Snail and the Whale' or Halloween favourite 'Room on the Broom'.

Look out too for the fab audio versions.

Available in a variety of formats and prices.

Illustration taken from The Gruffalo © Julia Donaldson and Axel Scheffler, 1999

GREAT FOR READING ALOUD ...

Aliens Love Underpants

by Claire Freedman and Ben Cort 🔊
ISBN 9781416917052   RRP £5.99

'Where do all your underpants go? Find out for yourself in this spectacular rhyming story that is perfect for reading aloud, and has some out-of-this-world pictures!'

Georgia Stanford,
Waterstone's Worcester
The Shambles

We're Going on a Bear Hunt

by Michael Rosen and Helen Oxenbury 🔊
ISBN 9780744523232   RRP £5.99

'Guaranteed to demand repeat readings from toddlers, this vivid and beautifully illustrated adventure story is a true chant-along classic with a great twist at the end.'

Sam Riedel,
Waterstone's Edinburgh
Ocean Terminal

Giraffes Can't Dance

by Giles Andreae and Guy Parker-Rees 🔊
ISBN 9781841215655   RRP £5.99

'Gerald is a clumsy giraffe who's not a very good dancer, but could he be listening to the wrong song? This is a fabulous book that will tickle your funny bone.'

Becky Hunt,
Waterstone's Worcester
The Shambles

Aaaarrgghh, Spider!

by Lydia Monks 🔊
ISBN 9781405210447   RRP £5.99

'Everything you'd want in a picture book; bright, bold illustrations, simple text and a friendly spider that just wants to be loved. My family adores it.'

Daniella Seaman,
Waterstone's Norwich Arcade

There Was an Old Lady Who Swallowed a Fly

by Pam Adams 🔊
ISBN 9780859530187   RRP £4.99

'The catchy rhyme, funny pictures and disgusting ending make this a guaranteed winner for reading aloud. You will definitely get a reaction.'

Sarah Williamson,
Waterstone's Tunbridge Wells

Hairy Maclary from Donaldson's Dairy

by Lynley Dodd 🔊
ISBN 9780140505313   RRP £4.99

'My children have consistently enjoyed 'Hairy Maclary' since they were a year old – my eldest is now five. The bouncy rhymes and memorable doggy characters make for great fun.'

Toby Bourne,
Waterstone's Children's Team

BEDTIME STORIES...

Russell the Sheep
by Rob Scotton 🔊
ISBN 9780007206223   RRP £5.99

'I adore this cute, quirky bedtime tale about endearing insomniac Russell. With exceptional illustrations and loveable characters, this is a must-read pre-slumber.'

Becky Jarvis,
Waterstone's High Wycombe

Peace at Last
by Jill Murphy
ISBN 9780230015487   RRP £5.99

'This classic picture book is an ideal bedtime story to read to young children – they will have great fun joining in making all the noises that keep Mr Bear awake.'

Janine Cook,
Waterstone's Gloucester

The Night Pirates
by Peter Harris and Deborah Allwright 🔊
ISBN 9781405211611   RRP £5.99

'Lovely rhythmic text and great illustrations make this story endlessly enjoyable. If your children are anything like mine you'll end up reading it over and over again – pirate impressions included!'

Daniella Seaman,
Waterstone's Norwich Arcade

The Kiss That Missed
by David Melling 🔊
ISBN 9780340797181   RRP £5.99

'This is a delightful bed-time story about a brave knight and a missing kiss. The pictures are full of exquisite detail; adults and children alike will love looking at them.'

Emma Cresswell,
Waterstone's Crewe

One Snowy Night
by Nick Butterworth 🔊
ISBN 9780007146932   RRP £5.99

'Percy is a kind-hearted soul – it's hard not to love him. The fabulous drawings and cosy story make this the perfect read to curl up together with on those cold winter nights.'

Rachael Bloxham,
Waterstone's Kirkcaldy

Owl Babies
by Martin Waddell and Patrick Benson 🔊
ISBN 9780744531671   RRP £5.99

'With memorable illustrations and a reassuring story of waiting for mum to return, this book will delight young children time and time again. One of the greatest picture books of all time.'

Vicky Hutchings,
Waterstone's Cardiff The Hayes

Ask a bookseller at Waterstones.com/ask

BOOKS FOR 3-5 YEAR-OLDS

kids' books

INTERACTIVE FUN...

The Jolly Postman

by Janet and Allan Ahlberg

ISBN 9780670886241   RRP £12.99

'So much more than just a book, this is based around favourite fairytales, but with hidden surprises and letters throughout. There is nothing but joy to be found here.'

Daniella Seaman,
Waterstone's Norwich Arcade

The Snowman

by Raymond Briggs

ISBN 9780140503500   RRP £6.99

'An all-time favourite story, told entirely in pictures. Each 'reading' can be adapted and personalised, lengthened or shortened, and is always magical. A must-have book for all children.'

Carol Dixon-Smith,
Waterstone's Windsor

Muddle Farm

by Axel Scheffler

ISBN 9781405020145   RRP £9.99

'Slide open the barn door and bring Farmer Muddle's busy farmyard to life. Create your own adventures with 15 animal magnets. Good imaginative fun and no need for wellies!'

Karl Whitmore,
Waterstone's Coventry Smithford Way

My Fairy Princess Palace

by Maggie Bateson and Louise Comfort

ISBN 9781405020763   RRP £14.99

'This fantastically pink and amazingly detailed pop-up fairy palace, complete with play-pieces, will provide hours of fun and excitement for any budding fairy princess.'

Tricia Jones,
Waterstone's Aberystwyth

Mixed Up Fairy Tales

by Nick Sharratt and Hilary Robinson

ISBN 9780340875582   RRP £6.99

'All your favourite fairytale characters are here, but YOU decide what happens. The story is never the same, and a giggle is guaranteed every time.'

Rachael Bloxham,
Waterstone's Kirkcaldy

Meerkat Mail

by Emily Gravett

ISBN 9781405090759   RRP £5.99

'This is one of my favourite picture books. Each page has so much going on that you can read it again and again, and always find something new and interesting.'

Meg Frost,
Waterstone's Card Team

22

PICTURE BOOKS FOR OLDER KIDS...

Full, Full, Full of Love

by Trish Cooke and Paul Howard
ISBN 9781844287826   RRP £5.99

'Join the fun as all the family come to Sunday dinner, there's a feast of food and plenty of love. An uplifting and reassuring story for all.'

Kate Philips,
Waterstone's Oxford

Commotion in the Ocean

by Giles Andreae and David Wojtowycz
ISBN 9781841211015   RRP £5.99

'With jolly, engaging verse and vibrant illustrations about the creatures that live under the sea, this is educational as well as entertaining.'

Alison Hay,
Waterstone's Derby University

Harry and the Bucketful of Dinosaurs

by Ian Whybrow and Adrian Reynolds
ISBN 9780140569803   RRP £5.99

'A simple, colourful story about Harry and his very unusual friends, who have some wonderful dinosaur names. Great fun to enjoy together.'

Tricia Jones,
Waterstone's Aberystwyth

Jamil's Clever Cat

by Fiona French
ISBN 9781845075187   RRP £6.99

'This sumptuously illustrated book is based on the Bengali version of the Puss-In-Boots story. I love the mosaic-style pictures; this is a joy to share with inquisitive children.'

Jenny Lee,
Editor

Diary of a Wombat

by Jackie French and Bruce Whatley
ISBN 9780007212071   RRP £4.99

'Beautifully illustrated, very funny and with a simple text, this Australian picture book is a firm favourite in my family. Eating, sleeping, digging holes... a wombat's work is never done!'

Gemma Harris,
Waterstone's Canterbury
St. Margaret's Street

The Selfish Crocodile

by Faustin Charles and Michael Terry
ISBN 9780747541936   RRP £5.99

'A clever, compassionate book that teaches children about the importance of sharing and friendship. The stunning illustrations help bring the story to life.'

Laura Sayers,
Waterstone's Merry Hill

PICTURE BOOKS FOR OLDER KIDS...

Library Lion

**by Michelle Knudsen
and Kevin Hawkes**
ISBN 9781406305678   RRP £5.99

'This adorable story of a
lion that wants to go to
the library is one of my
favourites. The exquisite,
nostalgic pictures make
this book a joy to read
and a gift to treasure.'

Jenny Lee,
Editor

Winnie the Witch

**by Valerie Thomas
and Korky Paul**
ISBN 9780192726438   RRP £5.99

'Winnie lives in a black
house, with black
furniture. She has a cat
called Wilbur who is also
black, so Winnie keeps
sitting on him! I love this
hilarious story about a
scatty witch.'

Hannah Liddell,
Waterstone's Redditch

The Tiger Who
Came to Tea

by Judith Kerr
ISBN 9780007215997   RRP £5.99

'Since this book was
first read to me, I wished
the Tiger would come
to my house for tea...
Perfect for stretching the
imagination, this still has
a special spot on my
bookshelf.'

Sarah Williamson,
Waterstone's Tunbridge Wells

The Very Busy Bee

by Jack Tickle
ISBN 9781845061630   RRP £7.99

'Toddlers love this fun
pop-up book about the
creepy-crawlies that
might be lurking
in their back garden.
With funny rhymes and
bold pictures this is
sure to become a
family favourite.'

Katie Waters,
Waterstone's Edinburgh West End

Six Dinner Sid

by Inga Moore
ISBN 9780340894118   RRP £5.99

'Every neighbourhood
has a Six Dinner Sid
tapping on the door
and asking for scraps.
This story is told with
wit and humour and
is accompanied by
beautifully realistic
pictures.'

Andrea Don,
Waterstone's Canterbury Rose Lane

All Afloat on
Noah's Boat!

**by Tony Mitton
and Guy Parker-Rees**
ISBN 9781846162428   RRP £5.99

'Joyful, colourful, rhyming
fun. Noah's story is
brought to life with the
leopards getting catty,
the rodents getting ratty
and the camels getting
the hump. You cannot
fail to love this!'

Shelley George,
Waterstone's Southampton
Above Bar

Sir Charlie Stinky Socks and the Really Big Adventure

by Kristina Stephenson
ISBN 9781405228039   RRP £5.99

'A crazy, rollicking take on the fairytale knight and his quest. With several fold-out pages, rambunctious illustrations and a hilarious story to boot, this is an exciting read.'

Helen Johnson,
Waterstone's University of East Anglia

Mog the Forgetful Cat

by Judith Kerr
ISBN 9780007171347   RRP £5.99

'Quite simply this is my absolute favourite picture book. Full of lovely illustrations, it is a great story of one VERY forgetful cat. A perfect bedtime story for under-fives.'

Jo Stanford,
Waterstone's Tunbridge Wells

Elmer

by David McKee
ISBN 9781842707319   RRP £5.99

'I love Elmer the patchwork elephant. This is a classic picture book that every child should own, because of the vibrant illustrations and cheeky humour of star of the show, Elmer.'

Arlene Crummy,
Waterstone's Newry

Click, Clack, Moo – Cows That Type

by Doreen Cronin and Betsy Lewin
ISBN 9780743461511   RRP £5.99

'Parents will enjoy the witty words whilst kids will love the funny cartoon pictures. Fun for every generation.'

Kim Retallack,
Waterstone's Plymouth
New George Street

Amazing Grace

by Mary Hoffman and Caroline Binch
ISBN 9781845077495   RRP £6.99

'Strong illustrations support a happy, hopeful story and show even the youngest reader that, regardless of colour, age or gender, you can be whatever you want to be.'

Kate Hames,
Waterstones.com Team

Dogger

by Shirley Hughes
ISBN 9780099927907   RRP £5.99

'We all remember how it feels to lose our most beloved toy, and this book perfectly captures that heartbreak. This is a lovely story of sibling kindness.'

Kirstin McCarle,
Waterstone's St. Andrews

Find local storytimes at Waterstones.com/events

BOOKS FOR 3-5 YEAR-OLDS

PICTURE BOOKS FOR EARLY READERS...

The Rainbow Fish

by Marcus Pfister
ISBN 9783314015441   RRP £5.99

'With entrancing, twinkly illustrations, this is an enduring tale about a little fish who learns about sharing and discovers the greatest gift of all, friendship.'

Sue Allen,
Waterstone's Merry Hill

The Lighthouse Keeper's Lunch

by Ronda and David Armitage
ISBN 9781407103150   RRP £5.99

'Filled with charming illustrations, this is a book that every child should grow up with. The story of some cheeky seagulls and poor Hamish the cat is a timeless bedtime favourite.'

Natalie Likness,
Waterstone's Staines

The Velveteen Rabbit

by Margery Williams
ISBN 9781405210546   RRP £5.99

'This classic picture book is packed with gorgeous illustrations to support a story that teaches children about overcoming loss, and the power of love.'

Carrie Innes,
Waterstone's Aberdeen Union Bridge

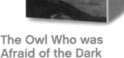

The Big Busy Book of Richard Scarry

by Richard Scarry
ISBN 9780007255016   RRP £8.99

'The brilliant, quirky pictures in this retro classic make this the perfect book to share with any child; you'll notice something different every time you read it.'

Kate Hancock,
Waterstone's Children's Team

The Owl Who was Afraid of the Dark

by Jill Tomlinson and Paul Howard
ISBN 9781405201773   RRP £5.99

'Kids of all ages will fall in love with baby owl Plop. This is an especially good read for children who don't want to sleep with the lights out.'

Beki David,
Waterstone's Grimsby

The Enormous Crocodile

by Roald Dahl
ISBN 9780141501765   RRP £6.99

'Get an early taste for the master storyteller with this snappy tale about a greedy crocodile. The longer paragraphs make this ideal for older kids too.'

Sarah Williamson,
Waterstone's Tunbridge Wells

BOOKS FOR 5-8 YEAR-OLDS

LEARNING TO READ...

Learning to read is one of the most significant stages in your child's development; parents often ask us about the process and how they can best support it at home. We asked expert **Ruth Miskin**, a former primary school headteacher and author of the **Read Write Inc** reading and writing programme (used in over 2,000 schools), to explain:

- At what age should a child start learning to read?
  It varies for each individual child, any time between the ages of three and five is fine.

- What are the main methods used to teach reading in schools?
  Schools have always used a mixture of phonics (working words out by sound-letter recognition) and 'look and say' (recognising and remembering words).
  The government now recognises that synthetic phonics is a good approach to learning to read. Schools must now teach children the 44 English speech sounds, and the various ways these can be represented by letters (e.g. p-l-ay, sh-ee-p, d-oor). Then children learn how to blend sounds together to read words.

- How can parents best support their child learning to read?
  Talk to your school about the schemes they are using. If it is synthetic phonics you can help teach your child to read the 44 sounds at speed, using flashcards.
  The most important way you can help is to give your child word power. Read anything and everything to your child; books, magazines, advertisements, cereal boxes – talk together all day. The more words they know and speak, the more they will understand in the books they will soon read for themselves.

- What should parents be looking for when buying reading scheme books or flashcards?
  Look for phonics flashcards that have memory prompts e.g. 'f' is turned into a flower.
  Choose lively books that children will be happy to read several times as they increase in speed and fluency.

READING SHOULD BE FUN!

LEARNING TO READ...

Read Write Inc

Available in various prices and formats

'Specially developed by synthetic phonics expert Ruth Miskin, with simple and engaging stories. These are a straightforward way to teach your child to read.'

Emma Wearn,
Waterstone's Southampton Above Bar

Jolly Phonics Reading Scheme

Available in various prices and formats

'The Jolly Phonics Reading Scheme covers all the ways a child learns, teaching via sounds, pictures and actions. Ideal for those with a shorter attention span, it's fun and has fast results.'

Helen Johnson,
Waterstone's University of East Anglia

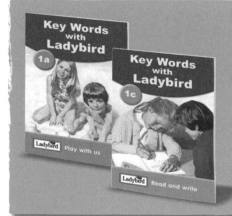

Ladybird Key Words Series

RRP £2.50

'This iconic reading scheme has taught generations of children to read. Peter and Jane's everyday stories are easy for kids to relate to and identify with.'

Katie Waters,
Waterstone's Edinburgh West End

Oxford Reading Tree
Read At Home Series

RRP £2.99

'This is perhaps the most comprehensive reading scheme available. Meticulously structured, there are plenty of books at each level to practise with before you move up.'

Karl Whitmore
Waterstone's Coventry Smithford Way

Oxford Reading Tree
Read At Home
Flashcards Word Games

RRP £5.99

'With a choice of four games and two levels of difficulty, these cards are perfect for the developing reader. Great for interactive play, and helping to develop confidence with language.'

Daniella Seaman,
Waterstone's Norwich Arcade

Ladybird Key Words Flashcards

RRP £3.99

'These flashcards are brilliant for teaching children new words and sentences. The double-sided cards are bold, clear and will not only help children to learn words, but to gradually structure sentences.'

Vicky Hutchings
Waterstone's Cardiff The Hayes

DEVELOPING READERS...

'Developing' is the stage at which children begin to read by themselves, moving from the hesitant deciphering of words to an assured understanding of sentences and paragraphs. It refers to the gradual build up of reading skills.

Kids at this stage need to practice their reading a lot, and it's important to ensure that the emphasis remains on reading for fun, as well as learning a vital life skill.

So what should you be looking for in books at this stage? We recommend books with large, clear print, short chapters and limited vocabulary. Look for lots of lively illustrations; these break up the story and help children interpret the meaning of the words.

Reading schemes such as the beautifully produced Usborne Young Reading Series and the colourful Bananas Reading Series match these criteria. There is a consistent level of vocabulary at each reading stage, making them ideal for practising and perfecting before moving up to the next level. Such schemes and early readers are a brilliant way to take your child through the steps to reading for themselves.

Finally, don't forget picture books. There is a particular delight in being able to go back and read for yourself a story that was read to you when younger!

Ladybird 'Read It Yourself' Series

RRP £2.50

'Perfect for encouraging confidence, Ladybird's range of reading materials are magnificent at developing essential reading skills in early readers. Divided into four progressive levels the 'Read It Yourself' series uses traditional tales to guide children through their first steps.'

John Lloyd
Waterstone's Bath

Usborne Young Reading Series

RRP £4.99

'These hardback books are delightful for developing readers. Each stage of reading difficulty is colour-coded to help you choose the right level for your child. There are plenty to choose from; be it dashing pirate stories or fascinating facts.'

Andrea Don,
Waterstone's Canterbury Rose Lane

Bananas Reading Series

RRP £3.99

'This is a simple, graded reading series in four stages with stories written by well-known authors. They are illustrated in colour and get progressively harder through the stages. The stories are great for building confidence before moving on to chapter books.'

Sarah Skinner
Waterstone's Norwich Castle Street

DEVELOPING READERS...

The Children Who Smelled a Rat

by Allan Ahlberg and Katharine McEwen

ISBN 9781406301342   RRP £5.99

'The delightful story of the Gaskitt family is perfectly matched by the hilarious illustrations. The short chapters and fast-paced shenanigans will keep young children entertained as they practise their reading skills.'

Kirstin McCarle,
Waterstone's St. Andrews

Happy Families Series

by Allan and Janet Ahlberg

ISBN 9780140312393   RRP £3.99

'I love this series. Based on the classic card game, it's a brilliant way to start children reading by themselves. Great illustrations and jolly stories make them both enduring and enjoyable.'

Daniella Seaman,
Waterstone's Norwich Arcade

Grandad's Dinosaur

by Brough Girling and Stephen Dell

ISBN 9780753410431   RRP £4.99

'Wonderfully colourful, with short chapters and a fun ending, this is a great book to hold the attention of a child progressing beyond picture books. Part of the popular 'I Am Reading' series.'

Hannah Barker,
Waterstone's Manchester Deansgate

Laura's Star and the Sleepover

by Klaus Baumgart

ISBN 9781845062071   RRP £4.99

'This gentle story captures the excitement and anxiety of staying away from home overnight. An ideal first read with its reassuring message and simple pictures.'

Jenny Lee,
Editor

The Witch's Dog

by Frank Rodgers

ISBN 9780140384666   RRP £4.99

'This imaginative story about a painting competition for witches' pets is sure to delight developing readers, with its simple language and numerous colourful pictures.'

Vicky Hutchings,
Waterstone's Cardiff The Hayes

Pirate School: Just a Bit of Wind

by Jeremy Strong

ISBN 9780141312699   RRP £4.99

'Jeremy Strong's hilarious books are great for younger readers. I love the illustrations – which break up the text so it looks less daunting, and the ridiculous names which make me giggle.'

Lisa Hunt,
Waterstone's Milton Keynes Silbury Avenue

AUDIO ...

Audio books help kids to enjoy stories that may be a little too complex for them to tackle on their own, and can provide hours of entertainment for everyone on long journeys. Younger titles have lots of fun sound effects and opportunities for children to join in, whilst older stories may be abridged so the story flows more swiftly. Look out for dramatisations, a great way to bring classic stories to life.

Look out for the (◄)) symbol throughout the guide, which indicates availability in audio format.

The Wheels on the Bus

ISBN 9781846071225   RRP £5

'All kids love to sing and this is a great way to get them started. Full of classic nursery rhymes and songs you can all join in with; it's great for helping with rhythm and speech development too.'

Daniella Seaman,
Waterstone's Norwich Arcade

rid Henry and Mega-Mean e Machine

Francesca Simon
d by Miranda
ardson
9780752872261   RRP £6.99

anda Richardson's
ant performance,
nplete with all the
erent voices and the
erbly funky sound
cts, makes this CD
ust-listen for kids
parents.'

Malkiewicz,
stone's Stirling

Five Go to Mystery Moor and Five on Kirrin Island Again

by Enid Blyton
ISBN 9781840326970   RRP £7.99

'Ah, the memories! The 'Famous Five' series was my favourite growing up and the mystery adventures still endure. This fully dramatised audio, complete with music and sound effects, is perfect for bedtime or long journeys.'

Arlene Crummy,
Waterstone's Newry

Real Fairy Storybook

by Georgie Adams and Sally Gardner
Read by Emma Chambers
ISBN 9780752861081   RRP £5.99

'This is a lovely collection of the stories that fairies tell to each other. Keep your little ones entertained with the escapades of these charming, cheeky creatures.'

Rachael Bloxham,
Waterstone's Kirkcaldy

CONFIDENT READERS...

'Confident Readers' refers to children who have mastered the basics of reading, and are now experiencing the pleasure of reading for themselves. Books in this section will have longer sentences and more developed vocabulary – yet still plenty of pictures. Younger books often consist of several short stories, whilst those aimed at older children will be complete novels with chapters.

Series fiction such as 'Beast Quest' and 'Rainbow Magic' comes into its own here, as kids like to know that the formula of a book they've loved is repeated in the next instalment. This gives children the comfort of the familiar, as well as the opportunity to strengthen their reading skills and develop a love of books – it's common to learn by repetition.

When choosing a book for kids at this stage, a good starting point is a theme or subject that reflects a child's interest or personality. Our booksellers have selected their favourite books covering all tastes: classic tales that have entertained successive generations, magical adventures, cute animals in peril, and budding secret agents. Gender-targeted books about sparkly princesses or fart-obsessed heroes tend to be particularly popular and are excellent for encouraging lighter readers. If you're not sure, please do ask a bookseller for their recommendations.

ANIMALS...

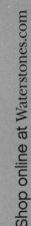

Sam the Stolen Puppy
by Holly Webb
ISBN 9781847150417   RRP £4.99

'Stories about pets are always popular at this age, and making it a detective mystery is genius! The short chapters are easy to pick up and put down, perfect for newly confident readers.'

Kim Retallack,
Waterstone's Plymouth New George Street

Animal Rescue Series
by Tina Nolan
ISBN 9781847150226   RRP £3.99

'This is a great series that will get any animal lover hooked. Filled with rabbits, puppies and kittens, the text is simple and the stories are absolutely adorable.'

Georgia Stanford,
Waterstone's Worcester The Shambles

The World According to Humphrey
by Betty G. Birney
ISBN 9780571226832   RRP £4.99

'Humphrey is a classroom hamster. His observations of children's lives at home and school, and the help he offers them, make for a funny, heart-warming book. Older readers will also enjoy this.'

Hattie Bevin,
Waterstone's Gloucester

Magic Kitten Series
by Sue Bentley
ISBN 9780141320168   RRP £3.99

'I really enjoy these stories, they have a magical quality about them. Aimed mainly at girls, the enchanted kitten Flame will capture their imagination and keep them reading.'

Emma Cresswell,
Waterstone's Crewe

Tumtum and Nutmeg
by Emily Bearn
ISBN 9781405233866   RRP £5.99

'Delightfully reminiscent of Enid Blyton and Brambly Hedge, these beautifully written and illustrated tales of adorable furry folk are the perfect bedtime story to share.'

Rachel Benn,
Waterstone's Children's Team

The Coldest Day in the Zoo
by Alan Rusbridger
ISBN 9780141317458   RRP £3.99

'Ever wanted to take an animal home from the zoo? In this amusing tale we see the comic consequences when the zookeepers do just that.'

Izzy Kertland,
Waterstone's Manchester Arndale

YOUNG ADVENTURERS ...

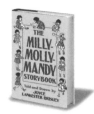

 (Utterly Me, Clarice Bean cover)

The Milly-Molly-Mandy Storybook

by Joyce Lankester Brisley
ISBN 9780753417096   RRP £8.99

'Several generations have enjoyed this series of classic village stories. With all the original illustrations and text, this beautifully produced hardback is the perfect nostalgia gift for new readers.'

Becky Hunt,
Waterstone's Worcester
The Shambles

Sophie's Adventures

by Dick King-Smith
ISBN 9781844289912   RRP £6.99

'Sophie is a rambunctious character children can really identify with. This bumper volume is packed with her lively animal-filled adventures.'

Tina Everitt,
Waterstone's Harrods

Utterly Me, Clarice Bean

by Lauren Child
ISBN 9781843623045   RRP £5.99

'Once you have read the Clarice Bean picture books you can enjoy this older story about her crazy family, teachers and friends. Laugh-out-loud funny, a great choice for any child.'

Beki David,
Waterstone's Grimsby

Clever Polly and the Stupid Wolf

by Catherine Storr
ISBN 9781903252284   RRP £6.99

'All the wolf wants to do is eat a little girl, but he has chosen one very clever girl, and he is unfortunately one very stupid wolf! A charming, classic tale.'

Jo Stanford,
Waterstone's Tunbridge Wells

Ottoline and the Yellow Cat

by Chris Riddell
ISBN 9781405050579   RRP £8.99

'This gorgous hardback is an enthralling read with a good mix of text and illustrations. The story is exciting and you'll love Ottoline's partner in crime, the small, hairy Mr Munroe.'

Meg Frost,
Waterstone's Card Team

Christophe's Story

by Nicki Cornwell
ISBN 9781845075217   RRP £4.99

'This moving story of a Rwandan refugee adjusting to life in England is a great way of helping young children learn about the wider world.'

Jenny Lee,
Editor

The Legend of Spud Murphy

by Eoin Colfer
ISBN 9780141317083   RRP £4.99

'This story of two mischievous boys, who meet their match in a terrifying librarian, will have you in fits of giggles. A wonderful story about the power of reading.'

Natalie Likness,
Waterstone's Staines

Cows In Action Series

by Steve Cole
ISBN 9781862301894   RRP £4.99

'The agents of the C.I.A. are time-travelling cows fighting against the evil F.B.I's (Fed-up Bull Institute) plots to change history. Hilarious, madcap historical chapter adventures for children aged five and over.'

Janine Cook,
Waterstone's Gloucester

Beast Quest Series

by Adam Blade
ISBN 9781846164835   RRP £4.99

'This exciting, action-packed adventure series has repeatedly won the hearts of less enthusiastic readers. With its simple prose but challenging vocabulary, it's a guaranteed winner.'

Tam Malkiewicz,
Waterstone's Stirling

Jack Stalwart Series

by Elizabeth Singer Hunt
ISBN 9781862301221   RRP £3.99

'Jet-setting secret agents, super gadgets and exotic locations! This brilliant series is a great place for curious kids to start reading on their own.'

Rachael Bloxham,
Waterstone's Kirkcaldy

The Boy with the Lightning Feet

by Sally Gardner
ISBN 9781842550878   RRP £4.99

'This is an inspiring, modern fairytale about a chubby boy who, with a little bit of magic, becomes a footballing sensation. This is a great confidence builder for young readers.'

Kate Tolhurst,
Waterstone's Stratford Upon Avon

Grandpa Chatterji

by Jamila Gavin
ISBN 9781405212854   RRP £4.99

'Neetu and Sanjay's grandpa is unlike any other; he makes amazing food and stands on his head! A funny story reflecting the difference between Indian and British life.'

Andrea Don,
Waterstone's Canterbury Rose Lane

BOOKS FOR 5-8 YEAR-OLDS – CONFIDENT READERS

HORRID HENRY

By Francesca Simon

Horrid Henry is rude, greedy, lazy, revolting, and yes, horrid! He is also hero to millions of children (dads quite like him too). Constantly getting into trouble at home and school, he likes nothing better than shouting and stomping, antagonising everyone he meets. Francesca Simon's anti-hero appeals to the rebel in every child.

Populated with instantly identifiable characters from Moody Margaret to Perfect Peter, each book contains several stories that are short, easy to read, and fast-paced. Tony Ross' zany illustrations capture the anarchy of the books, and best of all they are laugh-out-loud funny.

These gently subversive tales are fantastic, even for kids who don't read much, and are ideal for bridging the gap from developing to confident reader.

Look out too for the brilliant audio books read with mischievous glee by Miranda Richardson.

Illustration copyright © Tony Ross

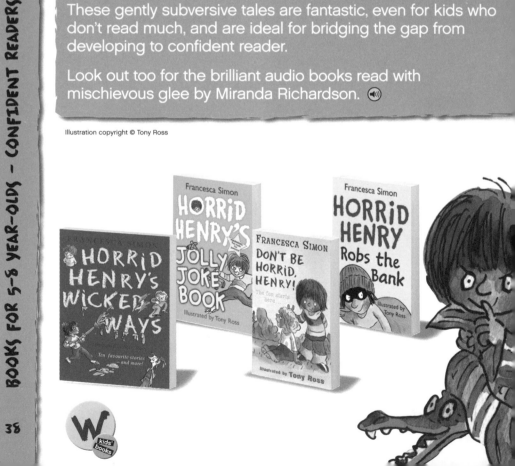

IF YOU LIKE HORRID HENRY, YOU'LL LOVE ...

You're a Bad Man, Mr Gum!

by Andy Stanton
ISBN 9781405223102   RRP £4.99

'Readers of all abilities will have great
fun reading this book about mean old
Mr Gum. This laugh-out-loud book has
lots of quirky illustrations that add to the
humorous story.'

Carrie Innes,
Waterstone's Aberdeen Union Bridge

Dirty Bertie: Burp!

by David Roberts and Alan MacDonald
ISBN 9781847150233   RRP £4.99

'With fantastic illustrations and brilliantly
funny stories fans of anything disgusting
will love Dirty Bertie. Younger readers
should also look out for the Dirty Bertie
picture books.'

Sarah Clarke,
Waterstone's Children's Team

My Naughty Little Sister

by Dorothy Edwards
ISBN 9781405233415   RRP £5.99

'This was my favourite as a child. Dorothy
Edwards' Naughty Little Sister must have
been based on my sister, because she
got up to things just like in the book!
Anyone with a sibling will identify.'

Andrea Don,
Waterstone's Canterbury Rose Lane

Jake Cake: The Werewolf Teacher

by Michael Broad
ISBN 9780141320878   RRP £3.99

'The writing and pictures in this book
are really endearing. The three short
stories follows Jake's rib-tickling series
of misadventures, encountering various
mythical creatures along the way.'

Sam Riedel,
Waterstone's Edinburgh
Ocean Terminal

BOOKS FOR 5-8 YEAR-OLDS – CONFIDENT READERS

TO MAKE YOU GIGGLE ...

Astrosaurs Series
by Steve Cole
ISBN 9780099472940   RRP £4.99

'With dinosaurs and spaceships, this fantastic series of books is perfect for younger readers looking for lots of silliness. The collectable cards at the back of each book are an added bonus.'

Davey Shields,
Waterstone's University of East Anglia

My Brother's Famous Bottom
by Jeremy Strong
ISBN 9780141322384   RRP £4.99

'The daft antics of a wacky family make this a chaotic, hilarious and totally fun read. I giggled my way from start to finish and you will too! Look out for the other books in the series.'

Carol Dixon-Smith,
Waterstone's Windsor

Arabel's Raven
by Joan Aiken
ISBN 9781903015148   RRP £4.99

'One of my all-time favourite books, this story of Arabel and her feisty pet raven Mortimer will have kids in stitches. I love the anarchic illustrations.'

Kate Hancock,
Waterstone's Children's Team

Stone Goblins
by David Melling
ISBN 9780340930489   RRP £3.99

'With toenail jam sandwiches, characters called Cheesyfeet and Saggypant, and heaps of suitably scruffy pencil sketches, young readers will enjoy wading through the sludgy, smelly, secret goblin world.'

Karl Whitmore,
Waterstone's Coventry Smithford Way

Spy Dog
by Andrew Cope
ISBN 9780141318844   RRP £4.99

'Lara is the dog world's answer to James Bond. The story of her attempt to go undercover as a family pet is a satisfying story for any animal-loving child who likes a bit of adventure.'

Alison Hay,
Waterstone's Derby University

Nelly the Monster Sitter
by Kes Gray
ISBN 9780340931912   RRP £4.99

'This is a fantastically imaginative story about resourceful heroine Nelly, and the monsters she babysits for. A laugh-out-loud series to really get your teeth into!'

Becky Jarvis,
Waterstone's High Wycombe

MAGICAL STORIES...

The Magic Faraway Tree

by Enid Blyton
ISBN 9781405240925   RRP £6.99

'The simple idea of different magical worlds appearing at the top of a tree has entranced generations of children. The Land of Treats was my favourite!'

Emma Wearn,
Waterstone's Southampton Above Bar

Flat Stanley

by Jeff Brown
ISBN 9781405204170   RRP £3.99

'Stanley can make himself so flat that he can post himself to faraway places in an envelope – my brother loved that part! Young readers will enjoy Stanley's unusual adventures.'

Arlene Crummy,
Waterstone's Newry

The Worst Witch

by Jill Murphy
ISBN 9780141314501   RRP £4.99

'Poor Mildred Hubble just can't seem to avoid getting things wrong, however hard she tries. Kids will enjoy identifying with her on her funny, hapless adventures.'

Jo Stanford,
Waterstone's Tunbridge Wells

Mrs Pepperpot Stories

by Alf Prøysen
ISBN 9780099411390   RRP £5.99

'Oh dear! Mrs Pepperpot's always shrinking, often at the wrong moment, but it doesn't stop her adventures or good deeds. These Scandinavian stories are ideal to share at bedtime or to challenge more confident readers.'

Sarah Williamson,
Waterstone's Tunbridge Wells

Magic Tree House Series

by Mary Pope Osborne
ISBN 9781862305236   RRP £3.99

'This imaginative, action-packed series follow a brother and sister through all sorts of adventures with different settings that will be recognised from school. Fantastic for fast-developing readers.'

Kate Phillips,
Waterstone's Oxford

The Little Prince

by Antoine de Saint-Exupery
ISBN 9780749707231   RRP £5.99

'Escape with the Little Prince to a beautiful universe where flowers talk and drawings come to life. Saint-Exupery's glowing drawings add to the dreamlike quality of this classic story.'

Helen Johnson,
Waterstone's University of East Anglia

BOOKS FOR 5-8 YEAR-OLDS – CONFIDENT READERS

RAINBOW MAGIC

by Daisy Meadows

This series of stories about two little girls rescuing fairies in peril have become the talk of the playground. The simple text, frequent illustrations and familiar format have made them an instant hit with 4–7 year-olds.

They capture every girl's dream of discovering fairies or magical powers. The traditional fairy has been updated; these are very modern types indulging in hobbies like roller-skating, tap dancing and netball. With a mixture of magic and glitter, each easily digestible chapter ends in a cliffhanger, which is perfect for bedtime reading.

Published in themed sets of seven, the Rainbow Magic books have a consistent level of language and vocabulary. These are brilliant books for encouraging children, particularly girls, to read.

© 2008 Rainbow Magic Limited. A HIT Entertainment company.Rainbow Magic is a trademark of Rainbow Magic Limited. Reg. U.S. Pat. & Tm. Off. And other countries.

HiT entertainment

IF YOU LIKE RAINBOW MAGIC, YOU'LL LOVE...

Fairy Dust

by Gwyneth Rees
ISBN 9780330415545   RRP £4.99

'Try this appealing tale of fairies and magic if you are looking for the next step beyond Rainbow Magic. With slightly longer chapters, but still plenty of illustrations, little girls will be enchanted by this sensitive and satisfying series.'

Amy Fox,
Waterstone's Southend

The Tiara Club Series

by Vivian French
ISBN 9781843628637   RRP £3.99

'These stories about princesses, balls and tiaras will delight little girls everywhere. Perfect for fans of all things pink.'

Laura Sayers,
Waterstone's Merry Hill

The Enchanted Horse

by Magdalen Nabb
ISBN 9780006747215   RRP £3.99

'Enter into the magical, secret world of Irina's imagination. This lovely book really touched my heart and is perfect for thoughtful young daydreamers.'

Shelley George,
Waterstone's Southampton Above Bar

The Tail of Emily Windsnap

by Liz Kessler
ISBN 9781842551660   RRP £5.99

'An enchanting, underwater adventure that's exciting and gripping to the last page. Emily is a feisty young girl who just happens to turn into a mermaid. Ideal for bridging the gap between 5-8 and 9-12 fiction.'

Hannah Liddell,
Waterstone's Redditch

FAIRYTALES AND MYTHS ...

The Three Little Pigs and Other Stories

by Stephen Tucker and Nick Sharratt

ISBN 9781405052399   RRP £10.99

'The wonderful illustrations in these lift-the-flap fairytale books give the traditional stories a fantastic modern day twist, whilst the witty verse is great to read aloud together.'

Meg Frost,
Waterstone's Card Team

The Fairy Tales

by Jan Pieńkowski and David Walser

ISBN 9780141382241   RRP £14.99

'A collection of well-loved fairytales are retold with beautiful silhouette illustrations. This book is a great gift for young and old alike.'

Carrie Innes,
Waterstone's Aberdeen Union Bridge

A Year Full of Stories

by Georgie Adams and Selina Young

ISBN 9781858816722   RRP £10.99

'With lovely colour illustrations, and a short poem or story for every day of the year, this is a brilliant book for bedtime reading.'

Justin Hutchinson,
Waterstone's Children's Team

The Orchard Book of Aesop's Fables

by Michael Morpurgo and Emma Chichester Clark

ISBN 9781843622710   RRP £12.99

'I was read these stories at bedtime as a child. Kids today can enjoy them with this marvellous retelling from Michael Morpurgo.'

Manel Awajan,
Waterstone's Lincoln

Greek Myths

by Marcia Williams   (RR)

ISBN 9781406303476   RRP £6.99

'From Hercules and his labours to Theseus, conqueror of the Minotaur, the exciting, enduring Greek Myths have been retold in a comic-strip form that makes them accessible to all.'

Hannah Liddell,
Waterstone's Redditch

Shakespeare Stories

by Leon Garfield and Michael Foreman

ISBN 9780140389388   RRP £12.99

'Leon Garfield has retold Shakespeare's plays as stories. With captivating illustrations, this is perfect for introducing children to the legendary playwright's work.'

Vicky Hutchings,
Waterstone's Cardiff The Hayes

POETRY ...

The Puffin Book of Fantastic First Poems

by June Crebbin
ISBN 9780141308982   RRP £7.99

'This wonderful collection of warm, funny, silly and surprising poems will engage and entertain young children who are moving on from nursery rhymes.'

Hattie Bavin,
Waterstone's Gloucester

Revolting Rhymes

by Roald Dahl
ISBN 9780141501758   RRP £7.99

'Horrible, nasty, disgusting and brilliant. Find out what Prince Charming is really like, and how naughty Little Red Riding Hood can be. A superb book that bridges picture books and poetry.'

Jo Stanford,
Waterstone's Tunbridge Wells

The Hutchinson Treasury of Children's Poetry

by Alison Sage
ISBN 9780091767488   RRP £19.99

'This is a really beautiful collection that includes lots of old favourites. The variety of illustration styles is impressive and makes this a book to treasure. The perfect gift.'

Kim Retallack,
Waterstone's Plymouth
New George Street

Mustard, Custard, Grumble Belly and Gravy

by Michael Rosen and Quentin Blake
ISBN 9780747587385   RRP £6.99

'This book of rambling, nonsense verse deserves to be read out loud to savour the sounds and silliness! Quentin Blake's zany illustrations only add to the fun.'

Emma Wearn,
Waterstone's Southampton
Above Bar

A Children's Treasury of Milligan

by Spike Milligan
ISBN 9781852273217   RRP £14.99

'Spike Milligan is the king of verse for children. Everybody will laugh-out-loud with mightily silly rhymes like 'On the Ning Nang Nong'. Whoever said that poetry was boring?'

Katie Waters,
Waterstone's Edinburgh
West End

Please Mrs Butler

by Allan Ahlberg
ISBN 9780140314946   RRP £4.99

'This collection of poems with their spot-on portrayal of primary school life, from picking teams to copycats, is the perfect introduction to poetry. I can still recite 'Dog In The Playground' by heart.'

Jenny Lee,
Editor

CLASSICS ...

Classics are a staple for any reader and book lover. These are the books that generations have known and loved. Puffin's use of popular modern authors and illustrators to design the covers and write the introductions brings their classics collection right into the 21st century.

Little Women

by Louisa May Alcott
ISBN 9780141321080   RRP £5.99

'An unashamedly girly read, with a fabbity fab new introduction from Louise Rennison, whose fans will adore it. I love this book to pieces and know that it would be my first choice for that mythical desert island.'

Sarah Skinner,
Waterstone's Norwich Castle Street

Wind in the Willows

by Kenneth Grahame
ISBN 9780141321134   RRP £5.99

'Wind in the Willows' is a simple tale of friendship and adventure that has stood the test of time incredibly well. I am never sure if Toad or Mole is my favourite character...'

Sarah Skinner,
Waterstone's Norwich Castle Street

Treasure Island

by Robert Louis Stevenson
ISBN 9780141321004   RRP £5.99

'Kids' favourite Eoin Colfer provides the introduction for this edition. Although this isn't the easiest of reads I do think it is the best pirate tale ever written.'

Sarah Skinner,
Waterstone's Norwich Castle Street

The Wonderful Wizard of Oz

by Robert Sabuda
ISBN 9780689834981   RRP £19.99

'Meet all the characters as they pop-up in this truly beautiful book. Readers will be entertained for hours.'

Kate Tolhurst,
Waterstone's Stratford Upon Avon

Pippi Longstocking

by Astrid Lindgren and Lauren Child
ISBN 9780192782403   RRP £14.99

'How gorgeous can one book be? Lauren Child's illustrations invigorate and perfectly complement the beloved story of eccentric Pippi and her mad-cap adventures.'

Kate Phillips,
Waterstone's Oxford

GREAT GIFTS ...

The Hutchinson Illustrated Treasury of Children's Literature

by Alison Sage
ISBN 9780091761448   RRP £19.99

'This magnificent treasury is the perfect introduction to children's books. Taking the reader from early rhymes to excerpts from older classics, everything you could want is in this one volume.'

Tam Malkiewicz,
Waterstone's Stirling

Gallop!

by Rufus Butler Seder
ISBN 9780761147633   RRP £9.99

'With scanimation technology bringing each page bursting to life, this book is fantabulous beyond belief; it keeps me entertained every time I flick through it. The turtle is my favourite!'

Becky Hunt,
Waterstone's Worcester
The Shambles

The Roald Dahl Treasury

by Roald Dahl
ISBN 9780224046916   RRP £19.99

'Packed with extracts from your favourite tales, this treasury captures the magic of one of our greatest storytellers. I think this is the perfect gift for kids.'

Gemma Harris,
Waterstone's Canterbury
St. Margaret's Street

'Ology' Series

by Dugald A. Steer   Available in a variety of prices and formats

'These fun and interactive books take topics such as dragons, pirates, history and magic to a whole new level. Full of maps, popups, stories, facts and artefacts to inspire enthusiasm, it is easy to lose whole days as you pore over these lavish books.'

Sarah Skinner,
Waterstone's Norwich Castle Street

Monsterology™ illustration copyright © 2008 Helen Ward.

BOOKS FOR 9-12 YEAR-OLDS

When children reach this reading age they are confident, competent readers. They are now ready for more elaborate sentence structures, complex plots, themes and sophisticated characterisations. Books will now help develop a child's language skills and vocabulary; stretch their imaginations, widen their horizons and encourage understanding of people whose lives are quite different from their own. Most importantly books can provide hours of unparalleled enjoyment.

Independent choice is important from now on, and there's plenty for kids to discover! It's important to let your child find his or her own way, as this is the perfect stage for them to try out lots of different genres and authors to discover which ones they like the most. Themes, subjects and familiarity are important here, and you may find your child can't get enough of one author, topic or style. Helpfully many authors write series or sets of similarly-themed novels.

There is something out there to captivate every child, and our booksellers have listed their top recommendations over the next few pages to help sustain and nurture reading interest.

For kids less engaged by reading, lookout for the ⓡⓡ symbol. The subject, layout, text and pictures in these books make them particularly accessible to reluctant readers.

RELUCTANT READERS ...

Some children, once they have learnt to read, subsequently lose interest in reading for fun. Boys in particular can overlook books as they grow older and other activities demand their time. Children that don't really enjoy reading are often referred to as 'reluctant readers'.

However, just because a child doesn't enjoy reading much now, it doesn't mean that they never will. Some children just don't like made up stories so do remember that proper reading doesn't just mean fiction; poring over a joke book or football magazine also involves interacting with words.

To help encourage reading, look for books with lots of humour; kids always enjoy books that feel a bit subversive or naughty. Choose books with a large typeface and short chapters as they are less daunting. Books with illustrations like graphic novels are another way to engage and hold interest, whilst audio books are an excellent way to help reluctant readers enjoy the same books as their friends.

Sometimes the reluctance to read may be symptomatic of a more specific problem. If you have concerns, you may want to talk to your child's teacher. Also see pages 112 – 113 for information on dyslexia and our partnership with Dyslexia Action.

Barrington Stoke

Barrington Stoke specialise in books for the reluctant, struggling or dyslexic reader of ages 8+. They have adapted the language, vocabulary, font, paper colour and layout of their books to minimise difficulties. They are designed to excite the reader, with gripping stories written by well-known authors, that combine suitable language for the reading age with content appropriate for the numerical age. There is something for everyone, and the books are clearly labelled to help you choose.

FAVOURITE CHARACTERS...

Doctor Who

Available in a variety of prices and formats

'The Doctor is a national treasure, and those of us who just can't get enough of the Time Lord can join him in the many books that accompany the TV series. From awesome activity books to stories of suspense, there is something for fans of all ages.'

Davey Shields,
Waterstone's University of East Anglia

Tintin

by Hergé   Available in a variety of prices and formats

'Packed with continuous action, adventure and a dark sense of humour, Tintin books are much more than just a children's comic series and will appeal particularly to less enthusiastic readers.'

Hattie Bavin,
Waterstone's Gloucester

Asterix

by Rene Goscinny and Albert Uderzo
Available in a variety of prices and formats

'These timeless tales of how Asterix, Obelix and their little Gaulish village repeatedly defy the Romans are packed full of visual jokes, witty dialogue and lots of action.'

Hannah Barker,
Waterstone's Manchester Deansgate

LIGHTER READS...

Pants Ahoy!

by Alan Snow (RR)

ISBN 9780192755407   RRP £5.99

'This is undoubtedly the silliest book you will ever read. It is also enormous fun, packed full of zany cartoons of our hero, the cabbage-heads and the adorable boxtrolls.'

Jenny Lee,
Editor

Goosebumps Series

by R.L. Stine (RR)

ISBN 9780439568463   RRP £3.99

'Spooky and sinister, this is a terrifying series about gruesome ghouls, living dummies and things that go bump in the night! Read them if you dare...'

Amy Fox,
Waterstone's Southend

The Adventures of Captain Underpants

by Dav Pilkey (RR)

ISBN 9780439014571   RRP £4.99

'Cheeky, naughty, and packed with amusing illustrations, this will capture the imagination of even the most unenthusiastic reader. Boys in particular will not want to put this book down.'

Kimberley Nevard,
Waterstone's Lakeside

Diary of a Wimpy Kid

by Jeff Kinney (RR)

ISBN 9780141324906   RRP £4.99

'This book made me laugh so much! What I really liked was that it was filled with expressive comic book style pictures that really show the trouble hero Greg gets into.'

Georgia Stanford,
Waterstone's Worcester
The Shambles

How to Train Your Dragon

by Cressida Cowell (RR)

ISBN 9780340860687   RRP £5.99

'I love this book about a trainee Viking and his stroppy dragon. It's laugh-out-loud funny and what's more – it was a young customer who recommended it to me!'

Katie Waters,
Waterstone's Edinburgh West End

Artemis Fowl: The Graphic Novel

by Eoin Colfer (RR)

ISBN 9780141322964   RRP £7.99

'This visually stunning graphic novel has all the trademark wit, humour and fantastical rip-roaring adventure of the original book and is ideal for less confident readers.'

Gemma Harris,
Waterstone's Canterbury
St. Margaret's Street

Free delivery to store at Waterstones.com

HARRY POTTER

by J.K. Rowling

Go through your contacts at random, phone them up and ask them to quickly name a kids' book… Was Harry Potter first to mind for most? We thought it might be! J.K. Rowling's series about the boy wizard, his friends, school, and trials and tribulations has been an unprecedented global publishing success story, with each new release greeted with enough anticipation and excitement to make any movie mogul green.

The reason for the popularity of the series is simple; Rowling has mixed in all the right ingredients of classic boarding school tale, mystery story and fantasy adventure. She really knows how to create a believable fictional universe, edge-of-your-seat tension and an oh-my-gosh-whatever-next plot. Of course, her true gift has been the creation of Harry himself, and Hermione, Ron, Hagrid and Dumbledore – all characters that kids (and adults!) can really root for, partly as they see a little bit of themselves in each one.

A great series to introduce kids to reading, the real challenge for many is: what to read now the series has stopped at book seven? Where else for the twists and turns, the magical environs and the against-all-odds adventures? Luckily there are plenty of such books; we've recommended a few here, but please do ask your local kids' bookseller for their favourites too.

IF YOU LIKE HARRY POTTER YOU'LL LOVE ...

Midnight for Charlie Bone

by Jenny Nimmo
ISBN 9781405225434   RRP £5.99

'I could not put this book down, it's absolutely riveting! The story takes you to a magical, humorous and dark world that younger Harry Potter fans will find a real treat.'

Alison Hay,
Waterstone's Derby University

Magyk

by Angie Sage
ISBN 9780747579267   RRP £6.99

'This first book in the fabulous series about Septimus Heap conjures up a wonderfully imaginative land with wizards, dragons and slightly scary baddies. Children of all ages will relish this.'

Victoria Furneaux,
Waterstone's Tunbridge Wells

Percy Jackson and the Lightning Thief

by Rick Riordan
ISBN 9780141319131   RRP £5.99

'Gods, monsters and heroes... what more could you ask for? I love Percy Jackson. An exciting mix of action and Greek mythology that gives Harry Potter a run for his money.'

Rachael Bloxham,
Waterstone's Kirkcaldy

The Shapeshifter: Finding the Fox

by Ali Sparkes
ISBN 9780192754653   RRP £5.99

'This is an excellent series about a boy discovering his ability to change into a fox. Soon he's sent off to a mysterious special school. The perfect mix of animals and magic.'

Tam Malkiewicz,
Waterstone's Stirling

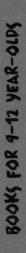
Free delivery to store at Waterstones.com

BOOKS FOR 9–12 YEAR-OLDS

MAGICAL FANTASY...

The Amulet of Samarkand

by Jonathan Stroud
ISBN 9780552550291   RRP £6.99

'This witty story about an apprentice magician is full of mayhem and mischief. It's a fantastic story with plenty of twists and turns, plus star turn, the wise-cracking djinni Bartimaeus.'

Beki David,
Waterstone's Grimsby

Inkheart

by Cornelia Funke
ISBN 9781904442219   RRP £6.99

'The magical possibility of making the imaginary real simply by reading aloud is surely every book lover's dream. This is a captivating and charming book, just right for kids that like to get lost in a story.'

Kirstin McCarle,
Waterstone's St. Andrews

Skulduggery Pleasant

by Derek Landy
ISBN 9780007241620   RRP £6.99

'This is a real page-turner; it had me hooked from the first word. A fantastically magical book with extraordinary characters, prepare to embark on an exhilarating adventure of wizardry and mayhem.'

Becky Jarvis,
Waterstone's High Wycombe

The Spook's Apprentice

by Joseph Delaney
ISBN 9780099456452   RRP £5.99

'This is the start of a genuinely dark, scary series about a boy who learns how to trap witches and boggarts. Heart-stopping and heartily recommended. Prepare to be 'spooked'.'

Karl Whitmore,
Waterstone's Coventry Smithford Way

Charmed Life

by Diana Wynne Jones
ISBN 9780007255290   RRP £5.99

'You will never get bored with this story about reluctant hero Eric, detestable Gwendolen, and a mysterious enchanter. Pure magic from a superb storyteller. '

Tina Everitt,
Waterstone's Harrods

Endymion Spring

by Matthew Skelton
ISBN 9780141320342   RRP £6.99

'This is a gripping read that brings together the lives of two boys born 600 years apart. Ideal for bookworms, this is an exciting and enthralling mystery.'

Shelley George,
Waterstone's Southampton Above Bar

OTHER WORLDS...

Ranger's Apprentice: The Ruins of Gorlan

by John Flanagan
ISBN 9780440867388   RRP £5.99

'This is 'Sword in the Stone' meets Harry Potter. Set in a magical, mystical era of knights and apprentices, this is the first book in a gripping action-packed series.'

Michelle Lever,
Waterstone's Bournemouth Castle Point

The City of Ember

by Jeanne DuPrau
ISBN 9780552552387   RRP £5.99

'Set in a not-impossible future, this novel asks: would you be brave enough to venture in to the unknown to save your city? An intelligent, engaging story that is full of thrills and spills.'

Hannah Barker,
Waterstone's Manchester Deansgate

Mister Monday

by Garth Nix
ISBN 9780007175017   RRP £5.99

"Mister Monday', by the always awesome Garth Nix, is full of suspense, mystery and adventure. It's the perfect bridge between younger stories and books the big kids read. You won't be disappointed by this series!'

Davey Shields,
Waterstone's University of East Anglia

The Lion, the Witch and the Wardrobe

by C.S. Lewis
ISBN 9780006716778   RRP £6.99

'I loved this book as a child. There is something extra special about seeing the imaginary world of Narnia through the eyes of the Pevensie children. This book is a real gem.'

Kim Retallack,
Waterstone's Plymouth New George Street

Troll Fell

by Katherine Langrish
ISBN 9780007170722   RRP £5.99

'This original fantasy novel cleverly uses Norse mythology to weave a sinister and beguiling modern fairytale. Will Peter escape before he is enslaved by the trolls forever?'

Katie Waters,
Waterstone's Edinburgh West End

Stoneheart

by Charlie Fletcher
ISBN 9780340911631   RRP £5.99

'The dark menace of London comes alive as George plunges into an epic adventure full of cinematic imagery, living statues and wonderful characters you can't help but cheer on.'

John Lloyd,
Waterstone's Bath

BOOKS FOR 9-12 YEAR-OLDS

FAERIES AND OTHER SMALL THINGS...

The Spiderwick Chronicles

by Holly Black and Tony DiTerlizzi
ISBN 9780689837388 RRP £6.99

'The Spiderwick Chronicles chart the adventures of the Grace siblings and their encounters with the goblins and boggarts that inhabit their aunt's house. With beautifully detailed illustrations, it's perfect for fledgling fantasy fans.'

Nyree Jillings,
Waterstone's Children's Team

Artemis Fowl

by Eoin Colfer
ISBN 9780141312125 RRP £6.99

'Unique, imaginative and hilarious, Artemis is a cool read for assured readers. Packed with vivid, exciting writing and fun characters, it's a real page-turning series.'

Kate Phillips,
Waterstone's Oxford

The Indian in the Cupboard

by Lynne Reid Banks
ISBN 9780007148981 RRP £4.99

'A charming story that captures your imagination, this has it all: cowboys, indians, magic, friendship and secrets. If you had a secret, who would you tell?'

Beki David,
Waterstone's Grimsby

The Tale of Despereaux

by Kate DiCamillo
ISBN 9780744598698 RRP £6.99

'A fairytale with a twist – unlikely hero Despereaux has the courage to believe in himself and save the princess from the rat-infested dungeon. An adorable tale for the whole family to enjoy.'

Sue Allen,
Waterstone's Merry Hill

The Various

by Steve Augarde
ISBN 9780552548588 RRP £5.99

'This is the first in a trilogy, and I promise you'll want to read them all. The story of a mystical tribe of little people has rich, colourful characters and plenty of humour.'

Shelley George,
Waterstone's Southampton Above Bar

The Borrowers

by Mary Norton
ISBN 9780140364514 RRP £6.99

'I can still remember having this read to me as a young child – one chapter every night. A classic adventure about the tiny folk who live under the floorboards.'

Janine Cook,
Waterstone's Gloucester

LAUGH YOUR PANTS OFF ...

The Killer Underpants

by Michael Lawrence (RR)
ISBN 9781841217130   RRP £5.99

'Meet Jiggy McCue, he attracts trouble like flies to something sticky! Jiggy's new underpants won't come off, and soon they start taking over his life. Perfect for less confident readers.'

Hannah Liddell,
Waterstone's Redditch

Just William

by Richmal Crompton (◀))
ISBN 9781405054577   RRP £5.99

'Naughty schoolboy William is a timeless character who wouldn't look out of place alongside today's favourites like Bart Simpson. The mischief and mishaps will have you giggling gleefully.'

Kirstin McCarle,
Waterstone's St. Andrews

A Series of Unfortunate Events

by Lemony Snicket (◀))
ISBN 9781405208673   RRP £6.99

'Numerous unfortunate events befall the Baudelaire children, yet these books are some of the funniest around, because of the wonderfully deadpan narrator and droll humour. Kids love them.'

Izzy Kertland,
Waterstone's Manchester Arndale

The Incredible Adventures of Professor Branestawm

by Norman Hunter
ISBN 9781862307360   RRP £5.99

'These silly short stories about Professor Branestawm's ridiculous inventions have lost none of their appeal over the years. Ideal for imaginative kids looking for something a bit different.'

Tina Everitt,
Waterstone's Harrods

Urgum the Axeman

by Kjartan Poskitt and Philip Reeve
ISBN 9781407102573   RRP £5.99

'By gum, you'll go wild for this side-splitting, superbly illustrated story about a tough, fearless barbarian struggling to contend with his feisty daughter, Molly.'

Karl Whitmore,
Waterstone's Coventry Smithford Way

The Falcon's Malteser

by Anthony Horowitz (RR) (◀))
ISBN 9781406300437   RRP £5.99

'Horowitz oozes wit and drama, the result of which is a fast-paced detective story which had me laughing on every page. I can't wait to read the next 'Diamond Brothers' book. '

Manel Awajan,
Waterstone's Lincoln

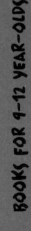

SCHOOL AND FRIENDSHIP ...

The Naughtiest Girl in the School
by Enid Blyton
ISBN 9780340917695   RRP £4.99

'Naughty Elizabeth is determined to get expelled from her new school. Does she manage it? Find out in this mischievous and entertaining tale.'

Amy Fox,
Waterstone's Southend

Malory Towers Series
by Enid Blyton
ISBN 9781405224031   RRP £4.99

'Anyone who reads these books will be begging to be sent to boarding school! Full of midnight feasts, practical jokes, friendships and lacrosse games, school has never been so exciting.'

Laura Sayers,
Waterstone's Merry Hill

The Invisible Friend
by Louise Arnold
ISBN 9780340892978   RRP £5.99

'This fantastic story understands how scary it can be starting a new school. It also takes a fresh approach to the supernatural; these endearing ghosts don't dress in sheets and rattle chains.'

Kim Retallack,
Waterstone's Plymouth New George Street

Flour Babies
by Anne Fine
ISBN 9780140361476   RRP £5.99

'This book is by turns funny and heart-warming. Following the story of a group of schoolboys assigned a rather unusual science project; it really makes you think about parenthood and babies.'

Sam Riedel,
Waterstone's Edinburgh Ocean Terminal

The Demon Headmaster
by Gillian Cross
ISBN 9780192753748   RRP £5.99

'Everyone thinks their headmaster is evil; this is the story of one who actually is! A thrilling and nail-biting story of the children who try to stop him.'

Lisa Hunt,
Waterstone's Milton Keynes Silbury Arcade

Stig of the Dump
by Clive King
ISBN 9780140364507   RRP £6.99

'I love this book because it fulfils every child's desire for fun and adventure. A glorious tale of an unlikely friendship, this will capture your heart and imagination.'

Becky Jarvis,
Waterstone's High Wycombe

ROALD DAHL

Roald Dahl has been one of the most popular children's writers for generations. Wonderfully, he can be enjoyed at every age, with picture books like 'The Enormous Crocodile', younger reads such as 'The Twits', classics like 'Matilda' and older short story collections such as 'Skin'.

We love Roald Dahl because he creates a world where kids rule! His young heroes and heroines always win the battles against adult injustice and oppression; Matilda's victory over Miss Trunchbull surely ranks as one of the most satisfying moments in kids' books. Dahl never talks down to his audience and his writing crackles with energy and the occasional made-up word!

Dahl's stories are subversive and wickedly funny. He creates a wonderland of wildly inventive plots and vivid characters, which are perfectly complemented by Quentin Blake's lively line drawings. Who hasn't longed to go to Willy Wonka's Chocolate Factory or meet the BFG? If you like stories you'll love Roald Dahl.

Available in a variety of prices and formats

AMAZING ADVENTURES...

The Famous Five Series

by Enid Blyton
ISBN 9780340681060 **RRP £4.99**

'Good old-fashioned mystery stories in which four children and a dog manage to solve crimes before the police do. With lashings and lashings of ginger beer, this is still beloved by contemporary kids.'

Sue Allen,
Waterstone's Merry Hill

Airman

by Eoin Colfer
ISBN 9780141383354 **RRP £10.99**

'This is a fantastic novel, and a huge departure from the more famous Artemis Fowl series. It is an action-packed tale that is part historical, part science fiction, and always totally enthralling.'

Sarah Skinner,
Waterstone's Norwich Castle Street

Swallows and Amazons

by Arthur Ransome
ISBN 9780099427339 **RRP £7.99**

'Join the Walker children on their perfect summer adventure, messing about in boats and on an island with no adults telling them what to do. A timeless children's classic.'

Justin Hutchinson,
Waterstone's Children's Team

A.N.T.I.D.O.T.E.

by Malorie Blackman
ISBN 9780552551687 **RRP £4.99**

'This gripping tale about a boy trying to prove his mum's innocence will capture your imagination from the first page. A fabulous, fast-paced thriller.'

Carrie Innes,
Waterstone's Aberdeen Union Bridge

Hatchet

by Gary Paulsen
ISBN 9780330439725 **RRP £4.99**

'This is an engrossing story about a boy having to survive on his own in the wild. Guaranteed to keep you on the edge of your seat.'

Meg Frost,
Waterstone's Card Team

Titanic 2020

by Colin Bateman
ISBN 9780340944455 **RRP £5.99**

'When Jimmy Armstrong stows away aboard a luxury cruise ship it's just the start of a gripping, futuristic tale involving a plague, mutiny and vicious, flesh-eating dogs. Unputdownable.'

Karl Whitmore,
Waterstone's Coventry Smithford Way

ANIMALS IN ACTION ...

The Hundred and One Dalmatians

by Dodie Smith
ISBN 9781405224802   **RRP £5.99**

'From scary Cruella de Vil to brave Colonel the Sheepdog, this wonderful book is a pleasure for all children. It's beautiful and heart-warming, I love it.'

Manel Awajan,
Waterstone's Lincoln

The White Giraffe

by Lauren St. John
ISBN 9781842555637   **RRP £5.99**

'An enchanting story combining myths, dreams and African wildlife, this book is perfect for anyone who wants an animal story with a difference.'

Carrie Innes,
Waterstone's Aberdeen Union Bridge

Wolf Brother

by Michelle Paver
ISBN 9781842551318   **RRP £6.99**

'This brilliantly realised adventure story, about the unique bond between a boy and a wolf in ancient times, is a favourite of mine. So real you can smell the forest!'

Rachael Bloxham,
Waterstone's Kirkcaldy

Doctor Dolittle Stories

by Hugh Lofting
ISBN 9780099265931   **RRP £6.99**

'Animal lovers will be enthralled by this story of wish fulfillment – being able to talk to animals. A simple idea brilliantly done.'

Sarah Williamson,
Waterstone's Tunbridge Wells

Varjak Paw

by S.F. Said
ISBN 9780552548182   **RRP £5.99**

'This captivating story mixes adventure and martial arts philosophy as Varjak embarks on a journey to save his family. Distinctive illustrations from Dave McKean help the story come to life.'

Kimberley Nevard,
Waterstone's Lakeside

The Little White Horse

by Elizabeth Goudge
ISBN 9780745945781   **RRP £4.99**

'A romantic children's classic about a feisty girl who sees a white horse, which she is convinced must be magical. Enchanting.'

Laura Sayers,
Waterstone's Merry Hill

ME AND MY PET...

Marley

by John Grogan
ISBN 9780007258048   RRP £5.99

'This is a story for all animal lovers. Everyone will fall in love with golden furball Marley, who's always getting into trouble!'

Natalie Likness,
Waterstone's Staines

A Dog Called Grk

by Joshua Doder
ISBN 9781842703847   RRP £4.99

'The adventures of resourceful Tim and his courageous dog Grk are ideal for action-loving children who are not quite old enough for the Alex Rider or Cherub series.'

Katie Waters,
Waterstone's Edinburgh West End

Mystic and the Midnight Ride

by Stacy Gregg
ISBN 9780007245192   RRP £4.99

'If you can't resist a bit of a tearjerker or a good horse story, this is for you. You'll be completely engrossed as Izzie trains her recalcitrant horse.'

Helen Johnson,
Waterstone's University of East Anglia

Animal Ark Series

by Lucy Daniels
ISBN 9780340944370   RRP £4.99

'If only these had been available when I was younger! They are poignant, funny, intriguing and uplifting. Perfect for less confident readers.'

Daniella Seaman,
Waterstone's Norwich Arcade

Hoot

by Carl Hiaasen
ISBN 9780330415293   RRP £5.99

'Featuring burrowing owls, a cast of oddballs and a school bully, this Florida-set crime story is easy to read and very funny.'

Meg Frost,
Waterstone's Card Team

The Great Elephant Chase

by Gillian Cross
ISBN 9780192753700   RRP £4.99

'How do you hide an elephant? That is the main challenge in this exciting, historical adventure. This is ideal for good readers looking for something a little different.'

Jenny Lee,
Editor

W kids' books

MICHAEL MORPURGO

Ace author of unique stories filled with warmth and poignancy, Michael Morpurgo is the perfect alternative to the numerous kids' fantasy and spy books.

He writes for all ages, covering an enormous range of subjects and settings. 'Kensuke's Kingdom' is a thrilling adventure story about shipwrecks and survival. 'War Horse' and 'Private Peaceful' are two of the most powerful books ever written about the First World War. 'The Butterfly Lion' is a magical tale about friendship, lions and Africa, whilst 'King of the Cloud Forests' is a mystical journey into the land of the Yeti. Present in all of them is Michael's deep love for nature, lyrical writing style and strong emotional impact.

This remarkable storyteller is perfect for keen readers from seven plus who are confident with language and ideas.

Available in a variety of prices and formats

WORLD AT WAR...

Goodnight Mister Tom
by Michelle Magorian
ISBN 9780140315417   RRP £5.99

'This is the touching story of a lonely boy's first taste of happiness when he is sent to live with grumpy Mister Tom during wartime. One of my all time favourites.'

Tricia Jones,
Waterstone's Aberystwyth

Hitler's Canary
by Sandi Toksvig
ISBN 9780440866626   RRP £5.99

'I was captivated by this poignant story about the Danish resistance with its memorable and quirky characters. An instantly engaging read, this story ended much too soon for my liking.'

Alison Hay,
Waterstone's Derby University

The Silver Sword
by Ian Serraillier
ISBN 9780099439493   RRP £4.99

'I first read this book while still at school and loved it. It is a timeless and compelling story of three Polish children's journey across war-torn Europe.'

Arlene Crummy,
Waterstone's Newry

The Machine Gunners
by Robert Westall
ISBN 9780330397858   RRP £5.99

'An incredibly captivating book set during the Second World War; the characters are well written and it's easy to immerse yourself in the story. Tense, thrilling and well worth the read.'

Tam Malkiewicz,
Waterstone's Stirling

I am David
by Anne Holm
ISBN 9780749701369   RRP £5.99

'A heartbreaking and humbling story about a boy's epic journey travelling across Europe in search of his mother. The ending is unforgettably powerful.'

Hannah Liddell,
Waterstone's Redditch

Rubies in the Snow
by Kate Hubbard
ISBN 9781904977735   RRP £5.99

'If you loved 'Anne Frank's Diary', this is one for you. This is a fictional tale of Tsar Nicholas' daughter Princess Anastasia's life in diary form, and it gives a fascinating insight into her world.'

Izzy Kertland,
Waterstone's Manchester Arndale

OTHER TIMES...

Roman Mysteries Series

by Caroline Lawrence (RR) (◀))

ISBN 9781842550205   RRP £6.99

absolutely adore The Roman Mysteries'. This exciting, enthralling adventure series meticulously covers every aspect of Roman life, from food and drink to chariot races. Everyone must read them!'

Kate Tolhurst,
Waterstone's Stratford Upon Avon

The Diamond of Drury Lane

by Julia Golding

ISBN 9781405237581   RRP £5.99

'The first of the brilliant Cat Royal books is an exciting and realistic romp through 18th century London. This was a deserving winner of the 2006 Waterstone's Children's Book Prize.'

Kate Hancock,
Waterstone's Children's Team

I, Coriander

by Sally Gardner (◀))

ISBN 9781842555040   RRP £6.99

'Mixing a gritty 17th century London with a dreamy alternative dimension, this is one of the most absorbing books I have ever read. Older readers will delight in this enchanting concoction.'

Jen Sattaur,
Waterstone's Aberystwyth

The Seeing Stone

by Kevin Crossley-Holland

ISBN 9780752844299   RRP £6.99

This well-researched book transported me instantly back to England at the time of the Crusades. With a compelling, slightly mystical element, I found this book and the three sequels unputdownable.'

Sarah Skinner,
Waterstone's Norwich Castle Street

Lady Grace Mysteries: A is for Assassin

by Grace Cavendish

ISBN 9781862303768   RRP £4.99

'This is the first in the excellent series about Lady Grace, a maid of honour at the court of Queen Elizabeth I. When Sir Gerald is murdered, it is Grace and her friends who solve the crime.'

Janine Cook,
Waterstone's Gloucester

Little House on the Prairie

by Laura Ingalls Wilder

ISBN 9780749709303   RRP £4.99

'A real gem of a classic, this is a moving and enthralling story about an American pioneer family. Great for kids who like a bit of reality in their adventure stories.'

Sarah Williamson,
Waterstone's Tunbridge Wells

Free delivery to store at Waterstones.com

BOOKS FOR 9-12 YEAR-OLDS

SPACE AND TIME ...

Cosmic

by Frank Cottrell Boyce
ISBN 9781405054645   RRP £9.99

'Quirky, touching and laugh-out-loud funny this fantastic book, about unusually tall Liam and the mishaps he gets into, is one of the best I've read in a very long time.'

Kate Hancock,
Waterstone's Children's Team

Gideon the Cutpurse

by Linda Buckley-Archer
ISBN 9781416916574   RRP £6.99

'Trapped in the 18th century, Peter and Katie soon make friends with a dashing highwayman. This is a brilliant time travel adventure, and has a jaw-droppingly shocking ending.'

Jenny Lee,
Editor

Tom's Midnight Garden

by Philippa Pearce
ISBN 9780192792426   RRP £5.99

'This is a wonderfully magical book that sticks with you, and keeps you listening out for that clock to strike thirteen. Terrific storytelling with a great twist.'

Lisa Hunt,
Waterstone's Milton Keynes
Silbury Arcade

George's Secret Key to the Universe

by Lucy and Stephen Hawking
ISBN 9780552559584   RRP £6.99

'Take a mad scientist and two young adventurers, throw in plenty of pictures and information, and you'll soon learn about the universe in this fun adventure.'

Carol Dixon-Smith,
Waterstone's Windsor

Charlotte Sometimes

by Penelope Farmer
ISBN 9780099433392   RRP £4.99

'This is an intriguing timeslip story set against the backdrop of the First World War. You won't be able to put it down because you'll be kept guessing right to the end.'

Helen Johnson,
Waterstone's University of East Anglia

The Number Devil

by Hans Magnus Enzensberger
ISBN 9781847080530   RRP £9.99

'Max, like many kids, hates maths. Then he meets the Number Devil, who helps Max and readers alike see that maths isn't boring at all.'

Andrea Don,
Waterstone's Canterbury Rose Lane

FAMILY LIFE ...

The London Eye Mystery

by Siobhan Dowd

ISBN 9780440868026   RRP £5.99

'When cousin Salim goes on the London Eye but never gets off, Ted and Kat have an unsolved mystery on their hands. Will Ted's unique way of thinking save the day?'

Becky Hunt,
Waterstone's Worcester City Arcade

The Penderwicks

by Jeanne Birdsall

ISBN 9780440867302   RRP £4.99

'I adore this contemporary story about the four Penderwick sisters, who spend their summer holiday getting into scrapes. This is a refreshing, bewitching book for assured readers.'

Jenny Lee,
Editor

Ways to Live Forever

by Sally Nicholls

ISBN 9781407105154   RRP £4.99

'You can't fail to be moved by this uplifting story about terminal illness. Honest and brave in its telling, this was a worthy winner of the 2008 Waterstone's Children's Book Prize.'

Beki David,
Waterstone's Grimsby

The Family from One End Street

by Eve Garnett

ISBN 9780141317168   RRP £6.99

'A children's classic about a family who know how to have fun. Each chapter contains a different adventure; these are super stories for children of all ages.'

Hannah Barker,
Waterstone's Manchester Deansgate

Saffy's Angel

by Hilary McKay

ISBN 9780340850800   RRP £5.99

'Enter the world of the colourful Casson family. Saffy's whole world is thrown into chaos when she discovers she's adopted. A fabulously quirky read that'll have you crying tears of sadness and laughter.'

Emma Wearn,
Waterstone's Southampton Above Bar

The Kick Off

by Dan Freedman

ISBN 9780439944304   RRP £4.99

'Jamie Johnson is football mad, and dreams of being the school's top player. His mum and teachers have other ideas. Sound familiar? Perfect for football fans everywhere.'

Davey Shields,
Waterstone's University of East Anglia

JACQUELINE WILSON

Jacqueline Wilson is one of the most popular kids' authors ever. Her genius is the uncanny knack of getting inside children's heads, convincingly capturing the voices and feelings of, particularly, young girls. The characters are so realistic they seem to jump off the page; Tracy Beaker, her most famous creation, is a fearsome mix of energy and attitude.

Wilson makes difficult situations like foster care and disability normal by treating them with humour, honesty and sensitivity. In 'The Suitcase Kid' Andy's parents get divorced and she longs for them to get back together, but there is no Hollywood reconciliation. Instead the story is about how Andy learns to cope with the new situation. In an imperfect world it's fantastic that there is an author willing to send out a realistic but positive message.

Older titles like 'Girls In Love' and 'Love Lessons' bridge the difficult gap between 9-12 and teen fiction, dealing brilliantly with the awkwardness of your friends changing around you and the desperate desire to fit in. Jacqueline Wilson is the author to grow up with.

Available in a variety of prices and formats

IF YOU LIKE JACQUELINE WILSON, YOU'LL LOVE ...

Scarlett

by Cathy Cassidy

(RR) (audio)

ISBN 9780141320229 RRP £5.99

'I love Cathy Cassidy and you will too. Read Scarlett's story and you'll soon see why. This is a story of love, growing up and friendship - you won't want it to finish.'

Natalie Likness,
Waterstone's Staines

32C That's Me

by Chris Higgins

ISBN 9780340917275 RRP £5.99

'Jess' perfect life is destroyed when her mum gets breast cancer, but her obsession with Lady Macbeth helps her cope. It had me crying and laughing all the way through.'

Andrea Don,
Waterstone's Canterbury Rose Lane

Deeper Than Blue

by Jill Hucklesby

ISBN 9781846163425 RRP £5.99

'Happy and sad, tragic and triumphant; I loved the characters, the story and the author's sense of humour. It was hard to put this book down. This is a brilliant read for Jacqueline Wilson fans looking for something a little more challenging.'

Carol Dixon-Smith,
Waterstone's Windsor

Ballet Shoes

by Noel Streatfeild

(audio)

ISBN 9780140300413 RRP £5.99

'If you long to shine like a star on the stage you'll love this quintessential story of the adopted Fossil sisters pursuing their dreams. You'll be wishing you were a Fossil – but which one?'

Emma Wearn,
Waterstone's Southampton
Above Bar

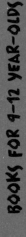

WIDER WORLD...

Journey to the River Sea

by Eva Ibbotson
ISBN 9780330397155   RRP £5.99

'The wonderfully exotic descriptions in this book make the Amazon come alive in your imagination. You will feel the sense of adventure and suspense until the very last word.'

Jo Stanford,
Waterstone's Tunbridge Wells

The Kite Rider

by Geraldine McCaughrean
ISBN 9780192755285   RRP £5.99

'There is something magical about this book, with its idea of a boy flying through the clouds on a kite. Filled with adventure, action and heroism, this is an astonishing novel about China.'

Georgia Stanford,
Waterstone's Worcester
The Shambles

The Breadwinner

by Deborah Ellis
ISBN 9780192752840   RRP £5.99

'This is an inspirational and insightful book, based on true stories of the brutality of the Taliban in Afghanistan. A great book for confident readers interested in the world around them.'

Arlene Crummy,
Waterstone's Newry

The Garbage King

by Elizabeth Laird
ISBN 9780330415026   RRP £5.99

'Set in Ethiopia, this compelling tale of poverty, determination, friendship and survival gives a fascinating insight into a different culture whilst also being a brilliant read.'

Hattie Bavin,
Waterstone's Gloucester

Spilled Water

by Sally Grindley
ISBN 9780747571469   RRP £5.99

'This is a powerful, emotional story set in China. With strong characters and simple but effective writing, this is a captivating book. '

Vicky Hutchings,
Waterstone's Cardiff The Hayes

Invisible City

by M.G. Harris
ISBN 9781407104027   RRP £6.99

'This is a poignant adventure story set in Mexico, about 13 year-old Josh who is struggling to accept his dad's death. With cleverly integrated blog entries, I found it exciting, fast-paced, and surprising right to the end.'

Emma Cresswell,
Waterstone's Crewe

BOOKS FOR TEENS

Teen fiction bridges the gap between children's and adults' books, recognising that teens have their own identity and interests, and want to read about other people like them.

Teen protagonists can be some of the most engaging characters in literature, and teen fiction is probably the most vibrant, innovative and daring genre within kids' books. The standard of writing is astonishingly good, with complex plots, demanding language and, sometimes, provocative content. Many of the most successful teen books deal with situations and emotions such as change, death and heartbreak that also appeal to an adult audience.

Books play an important part in teen culture, and at this stage many readers know which genres appeal to them – whether it is the mesmerising romance of Stephenie Meyer's 'Twilight' saga or the edgy thrillers of Robert Muchamore.

Mature younger children will also appreciate the complexity of plot and language in some teen books, particularly fantasy. However, teen fiction will always push the boundaries of acceptable content, and as far as possible we indicate here and in store the books you may find are not suitable for younger readers. Please do ask a bookseller for advice if you're unsure. Look for the ⑭ symbols here.

Ask a bookseller at Waterstones.com/ask

SPIES LIKE US . . .

Alex Rider Series

by Anthony Horowitz

Available in a variety of prices and formats

RR

'Alex Rider is a daring and charming (albeit reluctant) young spy who repeatedly saves the world. Each book is fast-paced, exciting and funny; perfect for thrill seekers aged 10+.'

Andrea Don,
Waterstone's Canterbury Rose Lane

Young Bond Series

by Charlie Higson

Available in a variety of prices and formats

'Meet the boy behind the legend. Brimming with hair-raising action, dastardly villains and exotic locations, the Young Bond books are spectacular spy adventures. Perfect for anyone who wants a satisfying and absorbing read.'

John Lloyd,
Waterstone's Bath

Cherub Series

by Robert Muchamore

RR

RRP £6.99

'No gadgets or über-villains here – what makes this series so addictively believable is its realistic and gritty portrayal of ordinary kids who work as spies. Teens of all reading abilities will whip through these cool, edgy books.'

Nyree Jillings,
Waterstone's Children's Team

KIDS VERSUS THE WORLD . . .

Jimmy Coates: Killer
by Joe Craig
ISBN 9780007196852   RRP £5.99

'Looking for action and adventure? Meet Jimmy Coates. Waking up to find you have powers you never had before is normally the stuff of dreams, but that's not the case for Jimmy...'

Kimberley Nevard,
Waterstone's Lakeside

Martyn Pig
by Kevin Brooks
ISBN 9781905294169   RRP £6.99

'Martyn is caught up in a nightmare that quickly spirals out of control. Gritty, funny, moving and shocking, Brooks is the master of powerful, gripping teen realism.'

Karl Whitmore,
Waterstone's Coventry Smithford Way

Girl, Missing
by Sophie McKenzie (RR)
ISBN 9781416917328   RRP £5.99

'A real page turner, filled with excitement, mystery, suspense and danger, this book taps into the feelings we all have as teenagers about who we are and where we belong.'

Hattie Bavin,
Waterstone's Gloucester

Flash Flood
by Chris Ryan (RR)
ISBN 9780099488637   RRP £5.99

'You'll be swept along by this fantastic adventure story. You'll be thrilled, scared and elated as Ben tries to survive in a flooded London.'

Tam Malkiewicz,
Waterstone's Stirling

Resistance
by Craig Simpson
ISBN 9780552555715   RRP £5.99

'Two brothers find themselves in the middle of the action in Nazi-occupied Norway. A gripping read about courage and loyalty, this is an adventure story with a conscience.'

Helen Johnson,
Waterstone's University of East Anglia

Blue Sky Freedom
by Gaby Halberstam (14+)
ISBN 9780330450515   RRP £5.99

'A powerful story set in the horrors of apartheid-ridden South Africa. Follow Victoria as she faces the trials of love and loss, and finds her courage and self-belief.'

Kate Phillips,
Waterstone's Oxford

HISTORICAL NOVELS ...

The Secret Countess
by Eva Ibbotson
ISBN 9780230014862   RRP £6.99

'Historical fiction is my favourite genre and this book fulfilled all the requirements: well-researched history, believable characters and a gentle love story. Teen girls will adore this.'

Sarah Skinner,
Waterstone's Norwich Castle Street

Between Two Seas
by Marie-Louise Jensen
ISBN 9780192755308   RRP £5.99

'I love this beautifully written and moving coming of age story about a girl's quest to find her father. Set in 19th century Denmark, this is full of romance, drama and self-discovery.'

Jenny Lee,
Editor

Newes from the Dead
by Mary Hooper   14+
ISBN 9780370329482   RRP £8.99

'Based on a true case, this is an excellent novel for the discerning reader. This fascinating and absorbing read tells the story of Anne's unfortunate life and the medical puzzle of her 'death'.'

Hannah Barker,
Waterstone's Manchester Deansgate

Remembrance
by Theresa Breslin
ISBN 9780552547383   RRP £5.99

'A passionately written tale of love, friendship, loss and pain during the First World War. Made more personal by the brilliant use of letters, I had to read this in one sitting. Utterly unforgettable.'

Carol Dixon-Smith,
Waterstone's Windsor

Witch Child
by Celia Rees
ISBN 9780747550099   RRP £5.99

'A gripping, thrilling novel that transports you to a time of paranoia and witch hunts. 'Witch Child' and the sequel 'Sorceress' are historical fiction at its very best.'

Sarah Clarke,
Waterstone's Children's Team

Stravaganza: City of Masks
by Mary Hoffman
ISBN 9780747595694   RRP £6.99

'This is an escapist fantasy set in the parallel worlds of renaissance Venice and contemporary Britain. The writing has a rich, lyrical quality and the plot is hugely imaginative.'

Nyree Jillings,
Waterstone's Children's Team

PHILIP PULLMAN

Philip Pullman is a master storyteller, capable of captivating readers of all ages with his rich prose and unforgettable, evocative imagery. He is most well known for 'His Dark Materials' trilogy (made up of 'Northern Lights', 'The Subtle Knife' and 'The Amber Spyglass'), the first part of which was filmed as 'The Golden Compass'.

Such is its wide appeal it's easy to forget that this genre-busting trilogy was originally written for older children. The reason for the books' popularity is that they work on two levels; most immediately, as enthralling adventure stories full of armoured bears and Texan hot air balloonists, but also as profound novels that raise and debate huge, important questions about love, innocence and religion. These are books to captivate, absorb and challenge. If you haven't read them yet, lucky you, the joy awaits!

Don't overlook Pullman's other great books; the Victorian quartet of novels about Sally Lockhart are page-turning detective fiction at its best, whilst his modern fairytales 'Clockwork' and 'I Was a Rat' are perfect for younger readers.

Available in a variety of prices and formats

Shop online at Waterstones.com

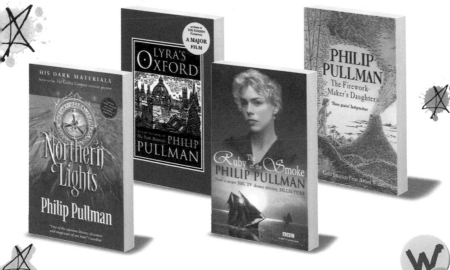

FANTASY ...

Eragon
by Christopher Paolini
ISBN 9780552552097   RRP £6.99

'This gripping fantasy will hook you from the very first page of the series. Follow the adventures of a simple farmboy as he learns to fly a dragon, battles evil and discovers his magical powers.'

Kimberley Nevard,
Waterstone's Lakeside

Sabriel
by Garth Nix
ISBN 9780007137312   RRP £6.99

'This is the explosive start to the magical 'Old Kingdom' series. Full of danger, death and destruction; Sabriel is a heroine you have to read about. I love it.'

Davey Shields,
Waterstone's University of East Anglia

Maximum Ride: The Angel Experiment
by James Patterson
ISBN 9780755321940   RRP £6.99

'Max is special, very special. Only 98% human, she is part of a sinister experiment. You will be instantly captivated by this highly original action-adventure.'

Laura Sayers,
Waterstone's Merry Hill

The Hobbit
by J.R.R. Tolkien
ISBN 9780006754022   RRP £6.99

'Tolkien's imagined world, its magical inhabitants and reluctant hero are brilliantly created. This is the original fantasy adventure story, and an essential read for any self-respecting fantasy fan.'

Kirstin McCarle,
Waterstone's St. Andrews

The Dark is Rising Sequence
by Susan Cooper
ISBN 9780140316889   RRP £14.99

'I was swept away in this glorious adventure story about the eternal struggle between good and evil. With four books in one, this is a classic read that will be treasured for life.'

Manel Awajan,
Waterstone's Lincoln

The Amazing Maurice and His Educated Rodents
by Terry Pratchett
ISBN 9780552552028   RRP £6.99

'Quite simply this is Pratchett at his best. You'll laugh, fall in love with street-smart Maurice and his rats, and be spellbound by their adventures. A great introduction to the master storyteller.'

Natalie Likness,
Waterstone's Staines

The Gift
by Alison Croggon
ISBN 9781844286362   RRP £7.99

'Maerad is a slave when she meets Cadvan and discovers her extraordinary destiny. This is one of the best fantasy books I have ever read, with strong characters and a plot that grips you from the first page.'

Tina Everitt,
Waterstone's Harrods

The Cry of the Icemark
by Stuart Hill
ISBN 9781904442608   RRP £6.99

'Left in charge of Icemark at the age of 14, Thirrin finds herself having to grow up quickly to protect her people. A winner of the Waterstone's Children's Book Prize, fans of classic fantasy will love this.'

Becky Hunt,
Waterstone's Worcester
The Shambles

Mortal Engines
by Philip Reeve
ISBN 9780439979436   RRP £6.99

'There is something for everyone in this utterly compelling and original story about moving cities, dashing aeronauts, killer robots and nefarious villains. This is my all-time favourite book.'

Jenny Lee,
Editor

Across the Nightingale Floor
by Lian Hearn
ISBN 9780330415286   RRP £6.99

'You will be captivated by this amazingly vivid and evocative tale of Japanese historical fiction. Find yourself lost in main character Tomasu's world and, who knows, you might not want to return.'

Sam Reidel,
Waterstone's Edinburgh
Ocean Terminal

North Child
by Edith Pattou
ISBN 9780746068373   RRP £6.99

'This wonderful retelling of Norwegian fairytale 'East of the Sun and West of the Moon' has it all: love, loss, adventure, magic and polar bears. The perfect novel to curl up with.'

Kate Hancock,
Waterstone's Children's Team

Ingo
by Helen Dunmore
ISBN 9780007204885   RRP £6.99

'The first in the series about the underwater world of Ingo, this is a mesmerising read. Ideally it should be read beside the sea. Once you start it you won't want it to end.'

Arlene Crummy,
Waterstone's Newry

URBAN GOTHIC...

The Twilight Saga

by Stephenie Meyer   Available in a variety of prices and formats

'If you are a teenage girl, and read only one thing, read this. Stephenie Meyer takes what could be a cliché, vampire romance, and turns it into something amazingly new and completely mesmerising. 'Twilight' is the first book in the series.'

Lisa Hunt,
Waterstone's Milton Keynes Silbury Avenue

Tithe

by Holly Black   (14+)
ISBN 9780689860423   RRP £6.99

'I was captivated by this world of faerie knights and their cold-as-ice queens. This magical world is sinister, unpredictable and often terrifying. Definitely for older teens, this is a great read.'

Shelley George,
Waterstone's Southampton Above Bar

A Great and Terrible Beauty

by Libba Bray
ISBN 9780689875359   RRP £6.99

'This compelling mix of mystery, romance and magic at a Victorian school will keep you hooked from the first page. Just wonderful.'

Carrie Innes,
Waterstone's Aberdeen Union Bridge

The Mediator Series

by Meg Cabot   (RR)
ISBN 9780330437370   RRP £5.99

'I love this series about no-nonsense teen-age ghostbuster Suze Simon. Has she met her match in gorgeous ghost Jesse? The fast-paced plot makes this a great read for younger teens.'

Jenny Lee,
Editor

Possessing Rayne

by Kate Cann   (14+)
ISBN 9781407102467   RRP £6.99

'This is a tense, spooky and romantic story about a sinister old house, from an always excellent author. It will keep you on the edge of your seat and jumping at shadows.'

Tina Everitt,
Waterstone's Harrods

HORROR ...

Darkside
by Tom Becker
ISBN 9780439944366   RRP £6.99

'I usually avoid books that seem scary, but I am so glad I made an exception for the fantastic 'Darkside'! I love this deserving winner of the 2007 Waterstone's Children's Book Prize.'

Sarah Skinner,
Waterstone's Norwich Castle Street

Darren Shan
Available in a variety of prices and formats   RR 🔊

'There is nothing better than Darren Shan for all those bloodthirsty horror fans. Combining breathtaking adventure with gruesome villains and unforgettable heroes his books sink their teeth into you and don't let go. Read at your peril.'

John Lloyd,
Waterstone's Bath

Raven's Gate
by Anthony Horowitz   RR 🔊
ISBN 9781844286195   RRP £6.99

'Warning: do not read this high-octane thriller after dark. The first in the 'Power of Five' series, this is a supernatural adventure that will send a chill down your spine and fear into your heart.'

Becky Jarvis,
Waterstone's High Wycombe

My Swordhand is Singing
by Marcus Sedgwick
ISBN 9781842555583   RRP £6.99

'Shrouded in mystery and intrigue, this is a sophisticated horror story that older teens will enjoy. The short, mesmerising chapters kept me gripped from start to finish.'

Emma Cresswell,
Waterstone's Crewe

The Devil's Footsteps
by E.E. Richardson
ISBN 9780552551717   RRP £5.99

'Moving shadows, dangerous places, ignorant adults and a shocking haunted house make this perfect for lovers of suspense and gore. Not for the faint-hearted!'

Hattie Bavin,
Waterstone's Gloucester

JUST FOR PLEASURE ...

Angus, Thongs and Full-Frontal Snogging

by Louise Rennison (RR) (♦))
ISBN 9780007218677   RRP £5.99

'Don't read this in public, as it will have you snorting out loud with laughter. Perfectly capturing teen life, you'll love this story of loony Georgia, her mad mates and even crazier family.'

Alison Hay,
Waterstone's Derby University

The Secret Diary of Adrian Mole Aged 13¾

by Sue Townsend
ISBN 9780141315980   RRP £5.99

'Totally timeless, Adrian's exploits are hilarious no matter how often you read this book. The ultimate teenage diary.'

Georgia Stanford,
Waterstone's Worcester
The Shambles

The Luxe

by Anna Godbersen
ISBN 9780141323367   RRP £6.99

'"Pride And Prejudice' meets 'The OC' in 19th century New York. This is the perfect piece of teen escapism – you won't be able to put it down.'

Kate Hancock,
Waterstone's Children's Team

My So-Called Life

by Joanna Nadin (RR)
ISBN 9780192755261   RRP £5.99

'Rachel longs for a dramatic life, but not much happens in Saffron Walden... I love this hysterically funny book, it provides an instant switch-off from school work.'

Jenny Lee,
Editor

The Princess Diaries

by Meg Cabot (♦))
ISBN 9780330482059   RRP £5.99

'Normal one minute, an official royal princess the next. Mia experiences (nearly) every girl's fairytale, only to find out it's just one more headache she doesn't need.'

Beki David,
Waterstone's Grimsby

Shiraz: Ibiza Diaries

by Grace Dent (RR)
ISBN 9780340970638   RRP £5.99

'Grace Dent's outrageous but loveable heroine Shiraz is off to Ibiza. The contemporary language and amusing storyline is sure to win over even the least enthusiastic teenage reader.'

Vicky Hutchings,
Waterstone's Cardiff The Hayes

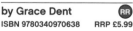

BOOKS FOR TEENS

OFFBEAT AND QUIRKY...

Stargirl

by Jerry Spinelli

ISBN 9781846165993   RRP £5.99

'Warning: this quirky, inspirational book could change your life. This beautifully written tale about individualism and daring to be different is a must-read for any (even secret) nonconformist.'

Nyree Jillings,
Waterstone's Children's Team

Holes

by Louis Sachar   RR 🔊

ISBN 9780747544593   RRP £6.99

'This was recommended to me when I first started working in a bookshop, and is now one of my favourite books. A truly life-affecting read, I get everyone I know to read it.'

Janine Cook,
Waterstone's Gloucester

Skellig

by David Almond

ISBN 9780340944950   RRP £5.99

'This is an enthralling story about an angel, who is dressed in black and eating spiders, when Michael stumbles across him. This is completely original and incredibly moving.'

Georgia Stanford,
Waterstone's Worcester
The Shambles

Elsewhere

by Gabrielle Zevin

ISBN 9780747577201   RRP £6.99

'The whole concept of death and the afterlife is so sensitively handled in this wonderful book that I truly hope Zevin is right about what happens when we die.'

Sarah Skinner,
Waterstone's Norwich Castle Street

The Declaration

by Gemma Malley

ISBN 9780747587743   RRP £6.99

'No-one knows what the future might hold, but Malley offers up a disturbingly plausible idea and asks does anyone have the right to decide whether one life is more important than another?'

Hannah Barker,
Waterstone's Manchester Deansgate

Keeper

by Mal Peet

ISBN 9781406303933   RRP £6.99

'Mal Peet is one of my favourite writers; he is a truly natural storyteller. 'Keeper' is an imaginative gem, merging a passion for football with an inspiring social message.'

Sam Riedel,
Waterstone's Edinburgh
Ocean Terminal

BOOKS FOR TEENS

PACKING A PUNCH...

Noughts and Crosses
by Malorie Blackman  14+
ISBN 9780552555708   RRP £6.99

'Blackman gives the Romeo and Juliet story an unexpected racial setting. The result is a deeply moving, dramatic, and thought-provoking book that every teen should read.'

Helen Johnson,
Waterstone's University of East Anglia

Life as We Knew it
by Susan Pfeffer
ISBN 9780439944335   RRP £6.99

'This is a terrifying but ultimately hopeful story about a family's attempt to survive in a world where the climate has dramatically changed. Horribly relevant, this is a brilliant, brilliant read.'

Jenny Lee,
Editor

Face
by Benjamin Zephaniah
ISBN 9780747541547   RRP £6.99

'A gripping book from the renowned political poet, 'Face' is a perceptive, poignant and compelling story about a horrific accident that changes a boy's life forever.'

John Lloyd,
Waterstone's Bath

Junk
by Melvin Burgess 14+
ISBN 9780141315935   RRP £6.99

'A groundbreaking and haunting book that looks at drug addiction from a teenager's point of view. It is powerful, disturbing and controversial, but above all it is brilliant.'

Jo Stanford,
Waterstone's Tunbridge Wells

The Chocolate War
by Robert Cormier
ISBN 9780141312514   RRP £6.99

'This book explores some really relevant teenage issues, including bullying and gang culture. It is a thought-provoking and often harrowing read, but thoroughly worth it.'

Sam Riedel,
Waterstone's Edinburgh
Ocean Terminal

(Un)arranged Marriage
by Bali Rai
ISBN 9780552547345   RRP £5.99

'This powerful story follows Manny between Britain and the Punjab as he fights against his family's arrangements for his marriage. An emotive story about identity, culture and tradition.'

Andrea Don,
Waterstone's Canterbury Rose Lane

COMING OF AGE ...

Let's Get Lost

by Sarra Manning 14+
ISBN 9780340877012   RRP £5.99

'Honest, gritty, fun and, at times, dark, this is easily one of my favourite books. The characters are complex and interesting, and the story is absorbing. Essential for teenage girls.'

Shelley George,
Waterstone's Southampton Above Bar

Broken Soup

by Jenny Valentine
ISBN 9780007229659   RRP £5.99

'Older Jacqueline Wilson fans will love this story about a family coming to terms with grief from an award-winning author. With wonderfully real characters, this is an irresistible read.'

Katie Waters,
Waterstone's Edinburgh West End

Just Listen

by Sarah Dessen 14+
ISBN 9780141322919   RRP £5.99

'Sarah Dessen is the undisputed queen of teen. This is an emotional rollercoaster of a read, dealing with first love, loss, betrayal and family turmoil. Teen fiction at its best.'

Hannah Liddell,
Waterstone's Redditch

Does My Head Look Big in This?

by Randa Abdel-Fattah
ISBN 9780439950589   RRP £5.99

'Amal has all the usual teen issues: boyfriends, mates, school and parents. She is also deciding whether to wear the hijab full-time. Funny and heart-warming.'

Mike Cooper,
Waterstone's Tunbridge Wells

Tamar

by Mal Peet
ISBN 9781406303940   RRP £7.99

'Tamar uncovers her family's secrets in this compelling coming of age story. Partially set against the backdrop of the Dutch Resistance during the Second World War, this is a magnificent novel for passionate readers.'

Sue Allen,
Waterstone's Merry Hill

Things I Know About Love

by Kate Le Vann
ISBN 9781853409998   RRP £6.99

'Diagnosed with leukaemia, Livia decides to visit America, hoping to learn about life and love. An emotional story about finding the positives in life, no matter what.'

Tricia Jones,
Waterstone's Aberystwyth

FOR GROWN-UPS TOO ...

The Boy in the Striped Pyjamas
by John Boyne
ISBN 9780099487821   RRP £6.99

'This is a tale that will stay with its readers forever. Nine year-old Bruno's simple story is incredibly powerful and completely unputdownable.'

Katie Waters,
Waterstone's Edinburgh West End

How I Live Now
by Meg Rosoff
ISBN 9780141318011   RRP £6.99

'This is one of the most compelling and original books I have ever read. It is a story of how love can survive even in the most extreme circumstances. Simply amazing.'

Jo Stanford,
Waterstone's Tunbridge Wells

The Princess Bride
by William Goldman
ISBN 9780747590583   RRP £6.99

'Not as soppy as the title suggests, this is a swash-buckling comic fantasy fairytale adventure with giants, magic and smart one-liners. This is my favourite book in all the world.'

Karl Whitmore,
Waterstone's Coventry Smithford Way

Coraline
by Neil Gaiman
ISBN 9780747562108   RRP £5.99

'Beautiful and haunting, Neil Gaiman writes in a humorous conversational style, making his fantasy all the more real. A masterful modern fable to be read by the flicker of candlelight.'

John Lloyd,
Waterstone's Bath

Before I Die
by Jenny Downham
ISBN 9781862304871   RRP £6.99

'The heartbreaking tale of Tessa, a 16 year-old with only a few months left to live. Incredibly well written, this story will stay with you for a very long time.'

Izzy Kertland,
Waterstone's Manchester Arndale

The Belgariad: Pawn of Prophecy
by David Eddings
ISBN 9780552554763   RRP £6.99

'Classic fantasy in the Tolkien vein, this is the first in a captivating, imaginative series that'll have you hooked. Superb characters, and great for exercising the muscle marked 'imagination'.'

Nyree Jillings,
Waterstone's Children's Team

FIRST ADULT

The move from the safety of kids' books to the extensive world of adult books can be difficult for even the most confident teen reader. Where do you start? We have selected here some of our favourite authors for you to try. They all offer an increased sophistication in plot, characterisation and ideas, yet remain approachable and appropriate reads for younger readers:

Douglas Adams – comic science fiction

Max Arthur – accessible history, look out for the 'Forgotten Voices' series

Bill Bryson – humorous travel writing

Trudi Canavan – fantasy

Agatha Christie – crime, the perfect start in this genre

Bernard Cornwell – historical fiction

Gerald Durrell – amusing autobiographies

Jasper Fforde – comic fiction

Robert Harris – thrillers; 'Fatherland' is particularly good

Georgette Heyer – witty romantic fiction

Susan Hill – fiction, look out for her seriously scary ghost stories

Nick Hornby – modern fiction, excellent for boys

Conn Iggulden – epic historical fiction

Sophie Kinsella – hysterically funny chick-lit

Daphne du Maurier – fiction, perfect for teen girls

George Orwell – fiction, brilliant, powerful and a must-read

Terry Pratchett – comic fantasy

Matthew Reilly – action thrillers

Alexander McCall Smith – light-hearted crime

Joe Simpson – adventurous travel writing

P.G. Wodehouse – comic fiction

John Wyndham – powerful science fiction

BOOKS FOR TEENS

NON-FICTION FOR KIDS

ACTIVITIES, HOBBIES AND REFERENCE...

Found in our stores under the banner of 'Reference', non-fiction covers everything from dictionaries and atlases to fun activity books and interactive encyclopedias. Some children prefer fact to made-up stories and, with a host of brilliant books to discover, this is the perfect place for curious kids to read about the world around them. Non-fiction books are also particularly good for engaging reluctant readers as the text is often broken up into snippets of information interspersed with pictures, rather than lots of daunting text.

We've divided up the following pages by subject themes rather than age, although we've included books to suit different age groups, where relevant, in every section. If you would like more recommendations, please a bookseller.

ACTIVITIES...

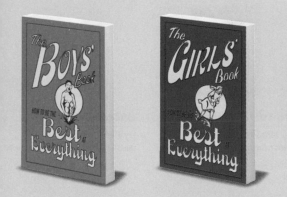

The Boys' Book and The Girls' Book

ISBN 9781905158645 and ISBN 9781905158799   RRP £7.99

'These books are fabulous. With loads of interesting facts and new things to learn, they will keep the kids away from the computer.'

Manel Awajan,
Waterstone's Lincoln

Where's Wally?

by Martin Handford
ISBN 9781406305890   RRP £5.99

'Tons of fun to be had searching for the little man in the hat. A timeless favourite and a sure hit for all ages.'

Kate Phillips,
Waterstone's Oxford

101 Things To Do Before You're Old and Boring

by Richard Horne and Helen Szirtes
ISBN 9780747580997   RRP £6.99

'This is full of great things to make and do for kids of all ages. Learn how to invent a secret code, make things glow in the dark and much, much, more.'

Gemma Harris,
Waterstone's Canterbury
St Margaret's Street

Fighting Fantasy Series

by Steve Jackson and Ian Livingstone (RR)
ISBN 9781840468076   RRP £4.99

'I love this series. Use a combination of luck and skill to foil fearsome foes and meet cunning challenges. Lose yourself in a book where you decide what happens next.'

Becky Jarvis,
Waterstone's High Wycombe

1001 Really Stupid Jokes

by Mike Phillips (RR)
ISBN 9781841191522   RRP £3.99

'A very funny joke book that kids will love. From stupid to stupider, these jokes are real crackers.'

Laura Dobbie,
Waterstone's Banbury

ACTIVITIES...

365 Things to Make and Do

by Fiona Watt
ISBN 9780746087923   RRP £12.99

'From finger-painting to Valentine's cards, this book is jam-packed with craft projects for every day of the year. Covering a variety of abilities, this will entertain the whole family.'

Tricia Jones,
Waterstone's Aberystwyth

Do You Doodle?

by Nikalas Catlow
ISBN 9781905158133   RRP £9.99

'This is no ordinary drawing book! This fantastic book makes you use your imagination and is guaranteed to give you hours of doodling fun whatever your age.'

Natalie Likness,
Waterstone's Staines

Ballerina

by Fiona Watt
ISBN 9780746076583   RRP £4.99

'A beautiful sticker book with a difference; dress the ballerinas with hundreds of stickers for different occasions, including performances of famous ballets. Great for keeping little hands busy.'

Gemma Harris,
Waterstone's Canterbury
St. Margaret's Street

Klutz Activity Kits

Available in a variety of formats and prices

'Klutz is huge fun for the whole family. Be it putting together a pirate ship or making amazing paper fashion, Klutz has something for everyone. The packs are very well put together and include everything you may need for your creative adventure.'

Tina Everitt,
Waterstone's Harrods

HOBBIES ...

Katie Meets the Impressionists

by James Mayhew
ISBN 9781860397684   RRP £5.99

The 'Katie' series makes art accessible to the very young with simple stories about great artists, and pictures rendered in the masters' styles. Stunning and inspirational.'

Jenny Lee,
Editor

The Art Book for Children

ISBN 9780714845111   RRP £12.95

'This is a fantastic book for older children to explore the world of art history, illustration and technique. Its vibrant presentation is guaranteed to keep their attention.'

Sue Allen,
Waterstone's Merry Hill

Big Book of Things to Draw

ISBN 9780746073711   RRP £9.99

'Learn how to draw anything from a pastel fantasy landscape to a waxy zebra. With simple, step-by-step instructions and tips on shading and perspective, it's ideal for budding artists looking for more detailed guidance.'

Karl Whitmore,
Waterstone's Coventry Smithford Way

Grow It, Eat It

ISBN 9781405328104   RRP £9.99

'This brilliant book tells you all you need to know to grow your own veg, and then how to turn them into a delicious meal you can eat. Parents and young children can enjoy this together.'

Sarah Williamson,
Waterstone's Tunbridge Wells

First Cookbook

by Angela Wilkes
ISBN 9780746078716   RRP £12.99

'A fantastic cookbook suitable for all ages. It covers all the basic skills you will need to learn, as well as a yummy variety of meals from Welsh rarebit to sticky chocolate cake.'

Janine Cook,
Waterstone's Gloucester

Cooking Up a Storm: The Teen Survival Cookbook

by Sam Stern
ISBN 9781844287741   RRP £9.99

'Tasty, well-explained recipes you'll be itching to try out on the rest of the family. Perfect for older kids eager to learn more than just the basics.'

Beki David,
Waterstone's Grimsby

HOBBIES

HOBBIES ...

Football: The Ultimate Guide (RR)

ISBN 9781405321860   RRP £12.99

'This really is the ultimate guide, packed full of info and stats on key club sides, national teams and all the best players from Sir Stanley Matthews to Fernando Torres.'

Jenny Lee,
Editor

Horse and Pony Factfile

by Sandy Ransford
ISBN 9780753413807   RRP £9.99

'This compact and informative factfile is great for quick reference and the perfect gift for any knowledgeable pony-lover.'

Hannah Liddell,
Waterstone's Redditch

Ballet Treasury

by Susannah Davidson and Katie Daynes
ISBN 9780746064160   RRP £9.99

'This is the perfect book for any little girl who dreams of being a ballerina. It includes a guide to the positions, synopses of the most performed ballets and biographies of famous dancers.'

Kirstin McCarle,
Waterstone's St. Andrews

Why Beethoven Threw the Stew

by Steven Isserlis
ISBN 9780571206162   RRP £4.99

'How do you interest modern kids in classical music? Tell them the outrageous stories about the composers found here and you will bring the great musicians and their music to life.'

Mike Cooper,
Waterstone's Tunbridge Wells

Looking After Your Pet Series

by Clare Hibbert
ISBN 9780750245203   RRP £6.99

'Covering everything from what to look for when choosing your pet, to how to feed and groom it, this easy-to-follow series will inform young children and encourage responsibility for their own beloved animal.'

Jenny Lee,
Editor

Starting Chess

by Harriet Castor
ISBN 9780746048306   RRP £4.99

'This beginner's guide will teach you all you need to know to win at chess. I gave it to my little sister and now regret it – she beats me every time!'

Gemma Harris,
Waterstone's Canterbury
St. Margaret's Street

GENERAL REFERENCE ...

Eyewitness Series

Available in a variety of prices and formats

'The 'Eyewitness' books are always so well laid out and interesting, they make it easy to learn something new. Covering a plethora of subjects, they are excellent, informative homework aids.'

Lisa Hunt,
Waterstone's Milton Keynes Silbury Arcade

Why Is Snot Green?

by Glenn Murphy (RR)
ISBN 9780330448529   RRP £4.99

'A fresh and funny take on science, providing comprehensive answers to all the silly questions that everyone thinks of but are too embarrassed to ask.'

Kirstin McCarle,
Waterstone's St. Andrews

Usborne Beginners Series

Available in a variety of prices and formats

'From frogs to firefighters, and pirates to planets, these books are a mine of information. A younger alternative to the 'Eyewitness' series, they are also brilliant books to read for fun.'

Hannah Liddell,
Waterstone's Redditch

The Book of Why

by Martine Laffon and Hortense De Chabaneix
ISBN 9780810959811   RRP £7.95

'Children are full of questions, and this book, which presents fascinating answers in a lively instructive way, will be a great help to any parent of an inquisitive young mind.'

Hattie Bavin,
Waterstone's Gloucester

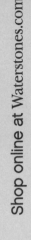

ENCYCLOPEDIAS AND DICTIONARIES...

Wow! RR

ISBN 9781405322485   RRP £19.99

'Wow! This book is exactly that. From cover to cover this is packed full of amazing information, presented in an innovative and attention-grabbing way. Ideal for knowledge-hungry kids aged seven plus.'

Michelle Lever,
Waterstone's Bournemouth
Castle Point

Oxford Dictionaries

Available in a variety of prices and formats

'I always recommend these authoritative dictionaries because they are clearly written and easy to understand. With versions tailored towards each age group from infant school to A-level students, they are the best way to guide your child through literacy.'

Andrea Don,
Waterstone's Canterbury Rose Lane

Collins Dictionaries

Available in a variety of prices and formats

'Compiled by a range of educational experts the Collins Children's Dictionaries have the needs of each and every pupil at heart. The younger illustrated dictionaries are colourful and easy to use, whilst the older students' titles also include built-in support with grammar and writing.'

John Lloyd,
Waterstone's Bath

The Oxford Illustrated Encyclopedia

ISBN 9780199104444   RRP £20

'Clear, concise and cleverly cross-referenced, this superb single volume encyclopedia will support your child through secondary school with authoritative entries on everything from Aborigines to Zoos.'

Karl Whitmore,
Waterstone's Coventry Smithford Way

LANGUAGES AND ATLASES ...

Usborne First Thousand Words Series

ISBN 9780746077627   RRP £6.99

'The friendly, bustling illustrations make learning your first thousand words in Chinese, Spanish, or any one of the other languages in the series. Very entertaining.'

Helen Johnson,
Waterstone's University of East Anglia

Adventures With Nicholas – French: The Missing Cat

ISBN 9789812468208   RRP £4.99

'With the new primary school focus on languages, this series is great for fun, additional home support. The stories are well supported by the CDs, making learning straightforward.'

Lisa Hunt,
Waterstone's Milton Keynes
Silbury Arcade

Oxford School French Dictionary

ISBN 9780199115280   RRP £5.99

'This little school French dictionary is ideal for more advanced language students. Easy to use with clear text and simple translations, plus there is a handy map of France inside. Also available in German and Spanish.'

Laura Dobbie,
Waterstone's Banbury

Picture Atlas
by Anita Ganeri

ISBN 9781405304078   RRP £12.99

'This brilliant junior atlas contains all you need to know about the world. From Everest to the Sahara, this atlas takes you on an instructive illustrated journey around our wonderful, varied planet.'

Kate Tolhurst,
Waterstone's Stratford Upon Avon

Philip's Modern School Atlas

ISBN 9780540087464   RRP £9.99

'This secondary school atlas is not only a source for maps, it is also an indispensable guide to the many varied topics that children study today, from pollution to exploration.'

Davey Shields,
Waterstone's University of East Anglia

Shop online at Waterstones.com

REFERENCE

OUR PLANET ...

A Life Like Mine

ISBN 9781405314602   **RRP £9.99**

'This is a fascinating look at the everyday lives of different children around the world. A great book for kids aged six and upwards who are curious about the world around them.'

Nyree Jillings,
Waterstone's Children's Team

The World Came to My Place Today

by Jo Readman and Ley Honor Roberts
ISBN 9781903919026   **RRP £5.99**

'When grandad comes to visit, George learns how everyday things like toys and chocolate bars come from all over the world. This wonderful picture book can be shared with very young readers.'

Laura Sayers,
Waterstone's Merry Hill

The Global Garden

by Kate Petty and Jennie Maizels
ISBN 9781903919163   **RRP £12.99**

'The Global Garden' is a beautifully presented, interactive book about the world of plants. This will fascinate children of all ages, whilst the educational content will delight parents.'

Vicky Hutchings,
Waterstone's Cardiff The Hayes

Spud Goes Green

by Giles Thaxton
ISBN 9781405217316   **RRP £5.99**

'This is a fun introduction, in diary form, to the importance of looking after our planet. Full of inspiring hints and tips, it's even made from recycled paper and printed with vegetable ink!'

Amy Fox,
Waterstone's Southend

Why Should I Bother About the Planet?

by Sue Meredith
ISBN 9780746089170   **RRP £6.99**

'This is the most straightforward introduction to climate change for children, and has lots of suggestions on how they can get involved and make a difference.'

Hannah Liddell,
Waterstone's Redditch

See Inside Planet Earth

by Katie Daynes and Peter Allen
ISBN 9780746087541   **RRP £8.99**

'Lift the flaps as you explore life on our planet. This is bursting with scientific and environmental facts presented in a fun and accessible way.'

Becky Jarvis,
Waterstone's High Wycombe

NATURE ...

Encyclopedia of Animals

by Jayne Parsons

ISBN 9781405315609   RRP £14.99

'This will answer all your animal-related questions. A comprehensive encyclopedia that takes you from Aardvark to Zebra in an explosion of colour and facts.'

Kimberley Nevard,
Waterstone's Lakeside

First Nature Book

by Minna Lacey

ISBN 9780746085158   RRP £7.99

'This is an ideal first introduction to wildlife, with lovely clear pictures, and lots of activities and information. It made me want to grab my wellies and go.'

Daniella Seaman,
Waterstone's Norwich Arcade

Bug Hunter

ISBN 9781405315128   RRP £7.99

'There is no excuse to stay indoors. This kit is amazing, it even has a bug-catcher for the slightly squeamish. The accompanying book is simple to use and easy to understand.'

Georgia Stanford,
Waterstone's Worcester
The Shambles

RSPB: My First Book of Garden Birds

by Sarah Whittley and Mike Unwin

ISBN 9780713676785   RRP £6.99

'This beautifully illustrated book is the perfect way to start learning about birds. With simple clues to help identify each bird, this book is ideal for young children.'

Natalie Likness,
Waterstone's Staines

Usborne Spotters Guides

ISBN 9780746073513   RRP £3.99

'This series encourages children to take an interest in the world around them. Each pocket-sized guide has spaces so you can tick things off as you spot them.'

Laura Sayers,
Waterstone's Merry Hill

Usborne Naturetrail Series

ISBN 9780746084045   RRP £7.99

'With a mixture of photographs and drawn illustrations, each guide is jam-packed full of information. Kids aged eight plus will be inspired to go on their own nature trails.'

Andrea Don,
Waterstone's Canterbury Rose Lane

REFERENCE

SCIENCE AND THE BODY ...

There's a House Inside My Mummy
by Giles Andreae
ISBN 9781841210681   RRP £5.99

'This invaluable book explains for younger children all the quirks of mum's pregnancy leading up to the happy event: why mum gets bigger, eats funny things and takes more naps.'

Beki David,
Waterstone's Grimsby

Growing Up
by Susan Meredith and Robyn Gee
ISBN 9780746031421   RRP £5.99

'Broken down into easy to follow chapters, with lots of clear illustrations, this explains the physical and emotional changes of puberty in a straightforward manner.'

Hannah Barker,
Waterstone's Manchester Deansgate

Flip-Flap Body Book
by Alistair Smith
ISBN 9780746033623   RRP £7.99

'This is a great book for young children. It has colourful, cartoon illustrations, mixed with simple text and flaps that lift to reveal what's happening inside your body.'

Emma Cresswell,
Waterstone's Crewe

Body
by Robert Winston
ISBN 9781405310420   RRP £12.99

'This book is just brilliant. It's colourful, informative and has some amazing illustrations. A fantastic reference book for older children that tells you everything you need to know about the human body.'

Alison Hay,
Waterstone's Derby University

The Glow in the Dark Book of Space
by Nicholas Harris and Vanessa Cabban
ISBN 9780711222557   RRP £10.99

'This is a children's reference book with a real difference. Having glow in the dark text, you can read all about the planets and stars in the dark!'

Carrie Innes,
Waterstone's Aberdeen Union Bridge

REFERENCE

Dorling Kindersley Celebrity Science

RRP £9.99

'These colourful books make seemingly dry facts exciting and interesting. Photographs and pictures help to illustrate the examples, which are taken from day-to-day life, so they are easy to follow and understand. This series is suitable for children aged eight upwards.'

Tina Everitt,
Waterstone's Harrods

The Usborne Internet-Linked Science Encyclopedia

by Judy Tatchell
ISBN 9780746053607   RRP £12.99

'An intelligent and invaluable resource, this useful encyclopedia provides a detailed reference for older kids with downloadable pictures, diagrams and website links.'

Sam Riedel,
Waterstone's Edinburgh Ocean Terminal

My Big Science Book

by Simon Mugford
ISBN 9781843321347   RRP £9.99

'With step-by-step instructions and colourful photographs, this is a great way for primary school kids to learn about science in a hands-on, fun way.'

Izzy Kertland,
Waterstone's Manchester Arndale

See How It's Made

ISBN 9781405319126   RRP £9.99

'All those ordinary things, that might not seem so interesting, take on a whole new life when you see how they are made. Featuring pencils, toothpaste tubes and even the book itself.'

Tam Malkiewicz,
Waterstone's Stirling

REFERENCE

HISTORY ...

Dinosaur Atlas

by John Malam
ISBN 9781405313438   RRP £12.99

'This has everything you need to know about dinosaurs in one bumper book, plus there's a fantastic CD-ROM full of activities. A must-have for the older dinosaur enthusiast.'

Rachael Bloxham,
Waterstone's Kirkcaldy

Dinosaurs

by Richard Dungworth
ISBN 9781840115987   RRP £12.99

'A perfect introduction to dinosaurs this is stuffed with enough facts and statistics to satisfy the most inquiring mind. Plus the scary pop-ups make the great lizards come alive.'

Andrea Don,
Waterstone's Canterbury Rose Lane

The Kingfisher History Encyclopedia

ISBN 9780753409756   RRP £25

'Whether it's intended for homework help or just dipping in-and-out of, this fully comprehensive, illustrated history of the world is an essential item for every child aged seven plus.'

Katie Waters,
Waterstone's Edinburgh West End

The Worst Children's Jobs in History

by Tony Robinson
ISBN 9780330442862   RRP £6.99

'Have you ever complained about doing the washing up or tidying your room (I bet you have)? Well, how would you like to be a Costermonger, a Piecer or even a Tooth Donor? Hmmm, thought not!'

Sarah Williamson,
Waterstone's Tunbridge Wells

A Street Through Time

by Anne Millard and Steve Noon   (RR)
ISBN 9780751355352   RRP £12.99

'This beautifully illustrated book is an alternative introduction to history, showing the development of a street over the centuries. Every time you look at the pictures, you see something new.'

Arlene Crummy,
Waterstone's Newry

The Usborne History of Britain
by Ruth Brocklehurst
ISBN 9780746084441   RRP £25

'This exceptional book gives you a complete overview of British history, covering everything from Anglo-Saxon fashion to the invention of railways. The perfect homework resource and an enthralling read for inquisitive minds.'

Jenny Lee,
Editor

See Inside Ancient Rome
by Katie Daynes
ISBN 9780746070031   RRP £8.99

'I love this book. Suitable for five to eleven year-olds, the style is great for little hands, whilst the content is still relevant for older children.'

Rachel Benn,
Waterstone's Children's Team

How to be a Knight
by David Steer
ISBN 9781840119282   RRP £12.99

'This beautifully presented gift book focuses on all aspects of how to succeed as a knight: from weapons and battles to building your own castle, this is great fun.'

Amy Fox,
Waterstone's Southend

Ticktock Essential History Guides
ISBN 9781846966552   RRP £4.99

'This series is full of bite-sized historical facts, mixed with photographs, illustrations, maps and timelines. These are perfect resources for projects and homework.'

Sarah Skinner,
Waterstone's Norwich Castle Street

The Danger Zone Series 🆁🆁
ISBN 9781904642763   RRP £5.99

'The 'Danger Zone' series have bright cartoon illustrations and just the right amount of information per page for kids to take in. They really bring the past to life.'

Kim Retallack,
Waterstone's Plymouth New George Street

The Diary of a Young Girl
by Anne Frank
ISBN 9780141315188   RRP £6.99

'Thought provoking and painfully sad, every child should read this diary that was never intended for publication. We can't change the past but a book like this can help us learn the lesson.'

Justin Hutchinson,
Waterstone's Children's Team

REFERENCE

HISTORY ...

Shop online at Waterstones.com

The 'Horrible' Series

by Terry Deary and Anita Ganeri
Available in various prices and formats

'The 'Horrible Histories' make history fun with their combination of cartoons, disgusting facts and jokes. They also give a great overview of all the key historical periods, and are incredibly informative. This winning formula has been expanded to cover Science, Maths, Geography, Football and Famous People.'

Jenny Lee,
Editor

My Story Series

RRP £5.99

'Falling perfectly between fact and fiction, this series of 'diaries' are historically accurate portraits of times and worlds that will fascinate, enthral and excite. A great way to engage older children with history.'

Rachel Benn,
Waterstone's Children's Team

RELIGION ...

Stories Jesus Told

by Nick Butterworth and Mick Inkpen

ISBN 9781859855881   RRP £7.99

'The authors of 'Percy The Park Keeper' and 'Kipper' have combined to create this simple introduction to the parables. Light, fresh and insightful.'

Jenny Lee,
Editor

The Children's Illustrated Bible

by Selina Hastings

ISBN 9781405303255   RRP £18.99

'This beautifully illustrated Bible is the perfect bible to grow up with. Added bonuses are the photographs and maps, which give the stories their historical context.'

Rodney Troubridge,
Waterstone's Marketing Team

A Child's First Book of Prayers

by Lois Rock and Alison Jay

ISBN 9780745944746   RRP £6.99

'There are over 150 prayers in this lovingly illustrated anthology. Easy to read and easy to enjoy, this superb collection is an ideal gift.'

Rachel Benn,
Waterstone's Children's Team

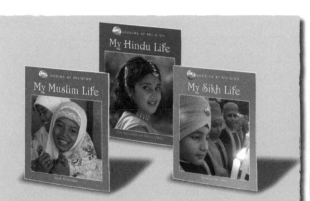

The Usborne Internet-Linked Encyclopedia of World Religions

by Susan Meredith and Clare Hickman

ISBN 9780746067093   RRP £9.99

'This beautiful book is a great introduction to the history and beliefs of the world's religions. You will find much to fascinate and educate in this all-inclusive book.'

Rachel Benn,
Waterstone's Children's Team

Looking at Religion Series

Available in various prices and formats

'What is it like being Hindu, Muslim or Sikh? This fantastic series has children from differing faiths explaining the beliefs, festivals, and rituals of their religion.'

Mike Cooper,
Waterstone's Tunbridge Wells

EDUCATION

STUDY GUIDES...

Books that help with a child's education at home is a popular subject with our customers. It's a seemingly confusing area, but with a brief explanation becomes much clearer.

The education system in England and Wales is structured around the National Curriculum which details the subjects and topics that should be taught, divided into age groups called Key Stages.

The National Curriculum can be supported at home by 'study guides' (a useful collective name for kids' education books). They are designed to be informative, practical and easy-to-use, and the great thing about them is that they are written by examiners or teachers so you can be sure your child is getting all the right information.

Within each Key Stage we have selected the best books to suit different requirements; books that stretch high achievers, make learning fun for the easily distracted, or help calm exam nerves. We have also included books for specific topics like handwriting and the National Tests.

Please do ask our booksellers for further recommendations, and your child's teacher will be happy to suggest suitable titles. With the right book and lots of encouragement, homework nightmares will become a thing of the past.

Please note that the educational systems in Scotland and Ireland have some key differences. For further information visit Waterstones.com, or see the Waterstone's Guide to Kids' Books bespoke versions for Scotland and Ireland.

PRE SCHOOL ...

Ages 3-5   **School Year:** Reception

These books are for learning all the important skills such as counting, opposites, colours, writing and shapes.

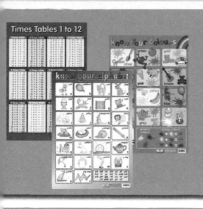

Chartmedia Posters

RRP £1.99

'Perfect for classrooms, kitchens and bedrooms these posters are bright and colourful and a sure fire way of helping kids to learn.'

Georgia Stanford,
Waterstone's Worcester The Shambles

Fun With Series

RRP £2.99

'The 'Fun With' books follow the National Curriculum and are ideal preparations for school. These easy-to-use guides keep learning fun and uncomplicated.'

Tina Everitt
Waterstone's Harrods

200 Maths and English Activities

ISBN 9781405496872   **RRP £7.99**

'With gold stars to help reward your child and fun illustrations, this series is perfect for early learning at home and makes some scary subjects seem a lot less confusing.'

Kate Hancock,
Waterstone's Children's Team

KEY STAGE 1...

Ages 5-7   **School Year: 1 and 2**

I Can Learn Series

RRP £4.99

'These are the perfect introduction to learning at home, with the bright, bold illustrations and fun characters that introduce the exercises. Parental notes offer additional support and understanding.'

Jenny Lee,
Editor

Letts Success SATS Series

RRP £3.50

'These books are clear, accessible and have just the right balance of learning and fun. Excellent for making the crossover from pre-school to school.'

Kate Phillips,
Waterstone's Oxford

CGP Study Book Series

RRP £3.95

'Sick of swotting? Bright, humorous and very easy to understand, these colourful study guides are brilliant at getting even the most reluctant student knuckling down to some revision.'

John Lloyd,
Waterstone's Bath

KEY SKILLS...

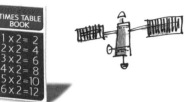

Foulsham Easy Times Table Book

ISBN 9780572009908   RRP £2.50

'Laid out with one table per page, you only need to learn the table that's highlighted – you've already learnt all the others! This makes times tables much less daunting.'

Andrea Don,
Waterstone's Canterbury Rose Lane

Andrew Brodie Mental Maths Series

ISBN 9780713670813   RRP £2.99

'This simple and effective series provides a clear approach to number work. Each book in the series encourages extensive practise of key maths skills – without a calculator.'

Jenny Lee,
Editor

Handwriting Today Series

by Andrew Brodie
ISBN 9780713671469   RRP £3.99

'These handwriting practise guides focus on improving existing skills for older children who need some help with technique and legibility. Added bonuses include the tips on spelling and presentation.'

Sarah Skinner,
Waterstone's Norwich Castle Street

Essential Spelling List

by Fred J Schonell
ISBN 9780174244936   RRP £3.50

'This is the perfect tool for brushing up on your spelling. It includes thousands of different everyday words, grouped together by type and difficulty.'

Mike Cooper,
Waterstone's Tunbridge Wells

KEY STAGE 2 ...

Ages 7-11   **School Year: 3, 4, 5, and 6**

Letts Success SATS Series

RRP £7.99

'Combining revision guides and practise papers, this excellent series will help your child grow in confidence when preparing for the SATS exams.'

Kate Hancock,
Waterstone's Children's Team

Letts Magical Topics Series

RRP £3.99

'If your child is finding it hard to concentrate on studying, these are the books to go for. Dragons and wizards are your guide, whilst there are lots of stickers and pictures to engage interest.'

Jenny Lee,
Editor

CGP Study Book Series

RRP £4.50

'Clear, motivational and tightly structured, these have long been one of the bestselling study series and deservedly so. The quirky jokes help keep study fun (almost).'

Kate Phillips,
Waterstone's Oxford

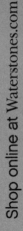

CGP Complete Revision and Practise Series

RRP from £9.99

'These approachable guides provide comprehensive revision notes in many subjects and at all levels. The entire syllabus is covered, but broken up into smaller segments, with worked examples to show exactly how to use the data.'

Sarah Skinner,
Waterstone's Norwich Castle Street

Letts Revise Series

RRP £9.50

'This series provides in-depth course coverage, frequent progress checks and practise questions. They also include tips from examiners on how to get higher marks.'

Rachel Benn,
Waterstone's Children's Team

Collins Easy Learning Workbook Series

RRP £3.50

'With lots of question practise and free online answers clearly showing the different levels, these study books provide the tools that a student needs for success.'

Kate Phillips,
Waterstone's Oxford

EDUCATION

NATIONAL TESTS...

Extra support is vital for major exams. These workbooks will help improve exam techniques.

CGP SATS Practice Papers

Available in a variety of prices and formats

'Each pack contains several full sets of different tests. Answers and an easy-to-use marking scheme are also included. Ideal for help in boosting your scores.'

Jenny Lee,
Editor

BBC Active Tests

RRP £9.99

'These study guides give you the real tests and marking schemes from previous years. A great way to ensure you feel confident and prepared when walking into the examination room.'

John Lloyd,
Waterstone's Bath

Letts SATS Papers

RRP £14.99

'Good all-round support for SATS preparation. The quick tests are great for timed practise and getting 'match-fit' for the exams.'

Kate Phillips,
Waterstone's Oxford

THE 11+ TEST ...

Most regions of the United Kingdom operate a comprehensive education system that is non-selective. However, a considerable number of local authorities, independent and private schools admit pupils based on selection, using an exam known as the 11+ Test.

The 11+ Test is taken in Year 6, the last year of primary school. Any of four areas can be tested: English, Maths, Verbal Reasoning (problem solving and processing text) and Non-Verbal Reasoning (problem solving and processing graphics/pictures). There is plenty of specialist help available for parents and children, from 'how to' books to practise test papers with strategies for improving scores.

There are two different formats for the test; standard or multiple choice. Your child's teacher will be able to advise which format is used in your area. If in doubt go for the standard test papers; these are fine to practise with as the child cannot guess so easily, even if the actual test is multiple choice.

These resources are also useful for those not sitting the 11+, as they offer practise in skills relevant to all pupils, and are a great way to stretch bright children.

Find out more at Waterstones.com/education

kids' books

THE 11+ TEST ...

Bond Papers

RRP £8.99

'This comprehensive range of books gives a solid grounding in the four basic skills and provide essential preparation and practise for the 11+, and other school tests.'

Rachel Benn,
Waterstone's Children's Team

Letts GL Assessment 11+ Practice Papers

RRP £9.99

'These practical, no-nonsense practice papers will help your child experience the exams at home. With a wide variety of packs, these will sustain regular practice sessions.'

Kate Hancock
Waterstone's Children's Team

Bond How to do Series

ISBN 9780748784967　　　　**RRP £9.99**

'This series will set even the most anxious mind at ease about the 11+, for it spells out what to expect, suggests strategies for success and contains detailed explanations on how to improve your performance.'

Jenny Lee,
Editor

HOMEWORK AIDS ...

Essential Facts and Tables

ISBN 9781864005240   RRP £2.99

'Packed full of multiplication tables, formulas, spelling rules and facts, this is an indispensable, instant homework resource for secondary school pupils.'

Jenny Lee,
Editor

Maths Dictionary

by Peter Robson

ISBN 9781872686189   RRP £2.95

'Explaining every mathematical word and phrase you could think of, this is a great point of reference whatever your mathematical ability. Clearly laid out with simple explanations and helpful examples.'

Hannah Barker,
Waterstone's Manchester Deansgate

The Periodic Table

by Adrian Dingle

ISBN 9780753415115   RRP £6.99

'Who ever thought science could be so cool? Manga style characters jazz up the periodic table, this is fun and informative for kids aged 10+.'

Rachael Bloxham,
Waterstone's Kirkcaldy

WHERE NEXT?

When 14 year-olds finish Key Stage 3, they are faced with picking their options for the GCSE exams.

Choosing Your GCSEs and Post-14 Options

ISBN 9781844551255   RRP £12.99

'This gives teens an informative analysis of the GCSEs and alternative qualifications available. It gives detailed insights into the links between subjects and career options, and will ensure students have all the information they need at their fingertips to make informed decisions about their future.'

Jenny Lee,
Editor

ABOUT DYSLEXIA ...

Dyslexia causes difficulties in learning to read, write and spell. Short-term memory, mathematical ability, concentration, personal organisation and sequencing may also be affected.

Dyslexia usually arises from a weakness in the processing of language-based information. Biological in origin, it tends to run in families, but environmental factors also contribute. Dyslexia can occur at any level of intellectual ability.

Dyslexia is not a disease and it cannot be cured. However, it is possible to help a dyslexic child learn to cope with and manage their difficulties, and reach their potential at school and beyond.

Dyslexia Action believes the best way to help a dyslexic learner of any age is through specialist tuition, with a trained teacher, that is tailored to meet the needs of the individual. What can be done will depend on individual circumstances and individual assessment is recommended.

For more information, help and advice please visit: **Waterstones.com/dyslexia** or **www.dyslexiaaction.org.uk**

Waterstone's and Dyslexia Action: working together to make reading enjoyable for all

At Waterstone's, we believe the joy of reading to be one of life's fundamental pleasures which should be able to be enjoyed by all. Waterstone's has supported Dyslexia Action since 2003 as our chosen charity because we both believe reading to be a vital and life-enhancing skill. For information on dyslexia and our partnership with Dyslexia Action go to: **Waterstones.com/dyslexia** or **www.dyslexiaaction.org.uk**

CHOOSING DYSLEXIA-FRIENDLY BOOKS FOR KIDS

Dyslexia is complex and affects different individuals differently; written text may not ever seem friendly for some, while others are avid readers! A good rule of thumb is, if a child is unable to read five or more words on a page it is fair to assume that this book is too difficult for them. They will spend all their time trying to read the words and not enjoying the actual story.

The specialists at Dyslexia Action use a grading system to assess the suitability of books which looks at the chronological age range for content that a child will enjoy matched to their reading age. However, any recommendation is subjective – individual tastes are still paramount – and grading isn't an exact science.

When you are choosing, Dyslexia Action recommends that you look out for the following:

- The **story is of interest** to the reader and relevant to his/her age.

- **Short sentences** and paragraphs – these help to maintain interest and encourage a feeling of progress.

- **Wide margins** and plenty of **white space** – these encourage a good reading flow and pace.

- **Right margins that aren't justified** as it is easier to distinguish between those lines read and those yet to be read.

- Books that have **pictures or headings** and other **signpostings where appropriate** as this helps navigation, and helps to break up text into manageable chunks.

- Books that are **printed on tinted paper** – this helps to reduce the resonance of black text on bright white paper, which can cause problems.

- Books that are printed in a **clear font** so that the letters are easily distinguishable, and in a clear print size of 11 point – but also not insultingly large for the intended age range.

DYSLEXIA

BOOKS THAT CAN HELP ...

We're often asked for books that can help on specific issues. Some common queries and suggestions are listed here. Please ask a Waterstone's bookseller for further advice and suggestions.

DEATH & BEREAVEMENT

Badger's Parting Gifts
by Susan Varley
ISBN 9780006643173   RRP £5.99

Picture book about the death of an old friend, and remembering him.

Goodbye Mog
by Judith Kerr
ISBN 9780007149698   RRP £5.99

Beautifully consoling picture book.

Michael Rosen's Sad Book
by Michael Rosen
ISBN 9781406313161   RRP £7.99

Moving picture book that gives an honest account of grief and sadness.

Waterbugs and Dragonflies
by Doris Stickney
ISBN 9780826464583   RRP £5.99

Practical book for explaining death, with religious overtones.

The Cat Mummy
by Jacqueline Wilson
ISBN 9780440864165   RRP £4.99

Coming to terms with the loss of a pet.

Truth About Forever
by Sarah Dessen
ISBN 9780141322926   RRP £6.99

Teen coming to terms with dad's death.

**For more information please try:
www.winstonswish.org.uk**

SERIOUS ILLNESS/GOING TO HOSPITAL

Harry and the Robots
by Ian Whybow and Adrian Reynolds
ISBN 9780140569827   RRP £5.99

Engaging picture book, helps to allay fears about going to hospital.

Going to the Hospital Sticker Book
ISBN 9780746099124   RRP £3.99

An 'Usborne First Experience' book for the very young.

Two Weeks with the Queen
by Morris Gleitzman
ISBN 9780141303000   RRP £4.99

Wonderfully down-to-earth novel about a sibling having cancer.

The Bower Bird
by Ann Kelley
ISBN 9781906307325   RRP £6.99

An award-winning novel about a teenage girl living with a rare heart condition.

For more information: www.winstonswish.org.uk

ADOPTION

My Parents Picked Me!

by Pat Thomas
ISBN 9780340910641   RRP £6.99

Sensitive picture book for young kids.

Saffy's Angel

by Hilary McKay
ISBN 9780340850800   RRP £5.99

Warm, funny novel about a girl discovering she is adopted.

BULLYING

Something Else

by Kathryn Cave
ISBN 9780140549072   RRP £4.99

Picture book about not excluding people because they are different.

Trouble at the Dinosaur Cafe

by Brian Moses and Gary Parsons
ISBN 9780140569940   RRP £5.99

Fun story for young kids about a bully taught the error of his ways.

The Angel of Nitshill Road

by Anne Fine
ISBN 9781405233200   RRP £4.99

Story about beating bullies at school.

Cloud Busting

by Malorie Blackman
ISBN 9780440866152   RRP £4.99

Powerful story for older kids about a bully and his victim.

Bullies, Bigmouths and So-Called Friends

by Jenny Alexander
ISBN 9780340911846   RRP £4.99

Practical book full of tip and strategies to beat bullying.

For more information please try: www.bullying.co.uk

DISABILITY

Susan Laughs

by Jeanne Willis & Tony Ross
ISBN 9780099407560   RRP £4.99

Picture book where the heroine is only revealed at the end to be in a wheelchair.

Private and Confidential

by Marion Ripley
ISBN 9781845070519   RRP £5.99

Picture book with a blind boy and a letter in Braille.

Red Sky in the Morning

by Elizabeth Laird
ISBN 9780330442909   RRP £4.99

Story for 9–12 year-olds about coming to terms with a disabled sibling.

Way I See It

by Nicole Dryburgh
ISBN 9780340956922   RRP £6.99

Inspiring autobiography for teens.

DIVORCE AND SEPARATION

Two of Everything
by Babette Cole
ISBN 9780099220626   RRP £5.99

Child-friendly introduction to divorce, ideal for young kids

Day with Dad
by Eva Eriksson
ISBN 9781406313840   RRP £10.99

A tender, straightforward picture book about a special day with Dad.

Help, Hope and Happiness
by Libby Rees
ISBN 9781905517022   RRP £9.99

Child's self help book for coping with divorce written by a teen author for other kids in her situation.

For more information: www.divorceaid.co.uk or www.itsnotyourfault.org.uk

GENDER ISSUES

And Tango Makes Three
by Justin Richardson, Peter Parnell & Henry Cole
ISBN 9781847381484   RRP £6.99

Picture book about two male penguins raising an egg together.

Hero
by Perry Moore
ISBN 9780552555869   RRP £5.99

Novel about gay teen with superpowers

The Perks of Being a Wallflower
by Stephen Chbosky
ISBN 9780671027346   RRP £6.99

Teen novel about a boy coming to terms with his sexuality.

Sugar Rush
by Julie Burchill
ISBN 9780330415835   RRP £5.99

Teen novel about lesbian love, serialised for TV.

LIFE IN THE UK

Gervelie's Journey
by Anthony Robinson & Annemarie Young
ISBN 9781845076528   RRP £11.99

This colourful picture book tells the true story of a child refugee from Africa for younger children.

Refugee Boy
by Benjamin Zephaniah
ISBN 9780747550860   RRP £6.99

Teen novel about an Ethiopian boy surviving on his own in London.

For more information: www.refugeecouncil.org.uk

The Colour of Home
by Mary Hoffman
ISBN 9780711219915   RRP £6.99

Picture book about a young boy adapting to life in England.

The Other Side of Truth
by Beverley Naidoo
ISBN 9780141304762   RRP £5.99

Novel about siblings fleeing Nigeria.

Boy Overboard
by Morris Gleitzman
ISBN 9780141316253   RRP £4.99

Humorous novel about a football-loving boy and his family fleeing Afghanistan.

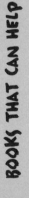

SPECIFIC ISSUES FOR YOUNGER KIDS...

NEW BABY

What's in Your Tummy Mummy
by Sam Lloyd
ISBN 9781843650911   RRP £6.99

Perfect for any toddler expecting a sibling.

Spot's Baby Sister
by Eric Hill
ISBN 9780140542882   RRP £4.99

Simple picture book for the very young.

Let's Talk About Where Babies Come From
by Robbie H. Harris
ISBN 9781844281732   RRP £9.99

A child-friendly illustrated, clear look at the facts of life.

POTTY TRAINING

Have You Seen My Potty?
by Mij Kelly and Mary McQuillan
ISBN 9780340911532   RRP £5.99

Hilarious picture book, perfect for potty training.

On Your Potty!
by Virginia Miller
ISBN 9781406311853   RRP £5.99

Encouraging picture book.

My Potty Book For Boys
ISBN 9781405311243   RRP £4.99

My Potty Book For Girls
ISBN 9781405311250   RRP £4.99

Practical, simple training books with sticker reward chart.

STARTING SCHOOL

Spot Goes to School
ISBN 9780140506501   RRP £4.99

Spot's first day at school is an exciting adventure.

I am Too Absolutely Small for School
by Lauren Child
ISBN 9781846168857   RRP £5.99

Fun, light-hearted picture book that sympathetically allays school fears.

Starting School
by Janet And Allan Ahlberg
ISBN 9780140507379   RRP £5.99

Ideal for calming anxieties.

Dinosaur Starts School
by Pamela Duncan Edwards and Deborah Allwright
ISBN 9781405035118   RRP £5.99

A reassuring picture book.

BEHAVIOUR

Little Book of Good Manners
by Christine Coirault
ISBN 9780954854805   RRP £7.99

Simple picture book introduction to good manners.

How Should I Behave?
by Mick Manning and Britta Granstorm
ISBN 9780749661182   RRP £5.99

A friendly, practical look at why good manners matter.

"I Don't Care"
by Brain Moses
ISBN 9780750221368   RRP £5.99

"It Wasn't Me"
by Brain Moses
ISBN 9780750221351   RRP £5.99

Fun series encouraging good behaviour.

FEARS AND FEELINGS

The Huge Bag of Worries
by Virginia Ironside
ISBN 9780340903179   RRP £5.99

Very useful picture book about not worrying.

No Matter What
by Debi Gliori
ISBN 9780747563310   RRP £5.99

Reassuring picture book about the strength of parents' love.

I Feel Sad
by Brian Moses
ISBN 9780750214063   RRP £5.99

I Feel Jealous
by Brian Moses
ISBN 9780750214056   RRP £5.99

I Feel Frightened
by Brian Moses
ISBN 9780750214049   RRP £5.99

I Feel Angry
by Brian Moses
ISBN 9780750214032   RRP £5.99

Fun series dealing with different emotions.

GENERAL FURTHER RESOURCES...

If you wish to seek out more in-depth help, please also see
www.childline.org.uk

PECIFIC ISSUES FOR TEENS...

SEX AND TEEN PREGNANCY

Forever
by Judy Blume
ISBN 9780330397803   RRP £5.99

Evergreen novel about sexual awakening.

Screwed
by Joanna Kenrick
ISBN 9780571239801   RRP £6.99

Graphically-portrayed novel about teen
sexuality.

Dear Nobody
by Berlie Doherty
ISBN 9780141311760   RRP £5.99

Moving account of teen pregnancy.

Megan
by Mary Hooper
ISBN 9780747541646   RRP £5.99

Supportive and informative view on teen
pregnancy.

Slam
by Nick Hornby
ISBN 9780141321400   RRP £7.99

Teen pregnancy from a boy's
perspective.

HEALTH AND CONFIDENCE

Go Ask Alice
by Anonymous
ISBN 9780099416371   RRP £6.99

A frank diary account of teen drug use.

Red Tears
by Joanna Kenrick
ISBN 9780571234837   RRP £6.99

A bold and candid novel about self-
harming.

Skin
by A.M Vrettos
ISBN 9781405223287   RRP £5.99

A moving novel about eating disorders
and the effect on family.

Fat Boy Swim
by Catherine Fforde
ISBN 9781405239660   RRP £6.99

Inspiring novel about fitness and
weight issues.

Stick Up For Yourself
by Gershen Kaufman
ISBN 9781575420684   RRP £9.99

Fantastic book for improving teen
self-esteem.

AUTHOR AND TITLE INDEX

1001 Really Stupid Jokes 87

101 Things to Do Before You Are Old and Boring 87

200 Gold Stars: Maths and English Activities 103

32c That's Me 69

365 Things to Make and Do 88

A

A.N.T.I.D.O.T.E 60

Aaaarrgghh, Spider! 20

Abdel-Fattah, Randa ...83

Across the Nightingale Floor 77

Adams, Georgie 33, 44

Adams, Pam 20

Adamson, Jean 9

Adventures of Captain Underpants, The 51

Adventures With Nicholas: The Missing Cat: French 93

Ahlberg, Allan 32, 45

Ahlberg, Janet & Allan 8, 22

Aiken, Joan 40

Airman 60

Alakija, Polly 9

Alcott, Louisa May 46

Alex Rider Series 72

Aliens Love Underpants 20

All Afloat on Noah's Boat! 24

Allen, Peter 94

Allwright, Deborah 21

Almond, David 81

Amazing Grace 25

Amazing Maurice and His Educated Rodents, The 76

Amber Spyglass, The ..75

Amulet of Samarkand, The 54

Andreae, Giles 20, 23, 96

Andrew Brodie Mental Maths Series 105

Angus, Thongs and Full-Frontal Snogging .80

Animal Ark Series 62

Animal Rescue Series 35

Arabel's Raven 40

Armitage, Ronda & David 26

Arnold, Louise 58

Art Book For Children, The 89

Artemis Fowl 56

Artemis Fowl: The Graphic Novel 51

Asterix 50

Astrosaurs Series 40

Augarde, Steve 56

Ayliffe, Alex 17

B

Baby Touch Series 6

Baby's First Cot Book 4

Baggott, Stella 4

Ballerinas 88

Ballet Shoes 69

Ballet Treasury 90

Bananas Reading Scheme 31

Banks, Lynne Reid 56

Bateman, Colin 60

Bateson, Maggie 22

Baumgart, Klaus 32

BBC Active Tests 108

Bearn, Emily 35

Beast Quest Seriesv 37

Becker, Tom 79

Before I Die 84

Belgariad: Pawn of Prophecy, The 84

Benson, Patrick 21

Bentley, Sue 35

Between Two Seas 74

BFG, The 59

Big Book of Things to Draw 89

Big Busy Book of Richard Scarry, The .. 26

Binch, Caroline 25

Birdsall, Jeanne 67

Birney, Betty G 35

Black, Holly 56, 78

Blackman, Malorie .60, 82

Blade, Adam 37

Blake, Quentin 18, 45

Blue Sky Freedom 73

Blyton, Enid **33, 41, 58, 60**

Body 96

Bond How to Do Series 110

Bond Papers 110

Bond, Michael 13

Book of Why, The 91

Borrowers, The 56

Boy in the Striped Pyjamas, The 84

Boy With Lightning Feet, The 37

Boyce, Frank Cottrell ..66

Boyne, John 84

Boys' Book, The 87

Bray, Libba 78

Breadwinner, The 70

Breslin, Theresa 74

Briggs, Raymond 22

Brisley, Joyce Lankester 36

Broad, Michael 39

Brocklehurst, Ruth 99

Brodie, Andrew 105

Broken Soup 83

Brooks, Felicity 9

Brooks, Kevin 73

Brown, Jeff 41

Brown, Margaret Wise ...8

Browne, Eileen 17

Buckley-Archer, Linda .66

Bug Hunter 95

Burgess, Melvin 82

Busy Airport 5

Butterfly Lion, The 63

Butterworth, Nick ..21, 101

C

Cabban, Vanessa 96

Cabot, Meg 78, 80

Calm Down Boris! 8

Campbell, Rod 8

Cann, Kate 78

Carle, Eric 17

Cassidy, Cathy 69

Castor, Harriet 90

Catch That Goat! 9

Catlow, Nikalas 88

Cavendish, Grace 65

CGP Complete Revision Series 107

CGP SATS Papers 108

CGP Study Book Series 104, 106

Chabaneix, Hortense De 91

Charles, Faustin 23

Charlie and Lola 12

Charlie and the Chocolate Factory 59

Charlotte Sometimes . 66

Charmed Life 54

Chart Media Posters .103

Cherub Series 72

Child, Lauren 12, 36, 46

Child's First Book of Prayers, A 101

Children Who Smelled a Rat, The 32

Children's Illustrated Bible, The 101

Children's Treasury of Milligan, A 45

Chocolate War, The 82

Christophe's Story 36

Cirque Du Freak 79

City of Ember, The 55

Clackety Clacks: Bee 4

Clark, Emma Chichester 44

Clever Polly and the Stupid Wolf 36

Click, Clack, Moo: Cows That Type 25

Clockwork 75

Coldest Day in the Zoo, The 35

Cole, Steve 37, 40

Colfer, Eoin ..37, 51, 56, 60

Collins Dictionaries 92

Collins Easy Learning Workbook Series 107

Comfort, Louise 22

Commotion in the Ocean 23

Cooke, Trish 23

Cooking Up a Storm: The Teen Survival Cookbook 89

Cooper, Susan 76

Cope, Andrew 40

Coraline 84

Cormier, Robert 82

Cornwell, Nicki 36

Cort, Ben 20
Cosmic 66
Cowell, Cressida 51
Cows in Action Series ..37
Craig, Joe 73
Crebbin, June 45
Croggon, Alison 77
Crompton, Richmal 57
Cronin, Doreen 25
Cross, Gillian 58, 62
Crossley-Holland, Kevin 65
Cry of the Icemark, The 77

D

Dahl, Roald ..26, 45, 47, 59
Danger Zone Series, The 99
Daniels, Lucy 62
Dark Is Rising Sequence, The 76
Darkside 79
Davidson, Susannah ...90
Daynes, Katie ...90, 94, 99
Dear Zoo 8
Deary, Terry 100
Declaration, The 81
Deeper Than Blue 69
Delaney, Joseph 54
Dell, Stephen 32
Demon Headmaster, The 58
Dent, Grace 80
Dessen, Sarah 83
Devil's Footsteps, The .79
Diamond of Drury Lane, The 65
Diary of a Wimpy Kid ...51
Diary of a Wombat 23
Diary of a Young Girl, The 99
DiCamillo, Kate 56
Dig Dig Digging 17
Dingle, Adrian 111
Dinosaur Atlas 98
Dinosaurs 98
Dirty Bertie: Burp! 39
Disney 11
DiTerlizzi, Tony 56
Do You Doodle? 88
Doctor Dolittle Stories .61
Doctor Who 50
Dodd, Emma 4

Dodd, Lynley 20
Doder, Joshua 62
Does My Head Look Big in This? 83
Dog Called Grk, A 62
Dogger 25
Donaldson, Julia 19
Dorling Kindersley Celebrity Science Series 97
Dowd, Siobhan 67
Downham, Jenny 84
Dr. Seuss 12
Dragonology 47
Dunbar, Polly 18
Dungworth, Richard 98
Dunmore, Helen 77
DuPrau, Jeanne 55

E

Easy Times Table Book, The 105
Eddings, David 84
Edwards, Dorothy 39
Egyptology 47
Ellis, Deborah 70
Elmer 25
Elsewhere 81
Enchanted Horse, The .43
Encyclopedia of Animals 95
Endymion Spring 54
Enormous Crocodile, The 26, 59
Eragon 76
Essential Facts and Tables 111
Essential Spelling List 105
Eyewitness Series 91

F

Face 82
Fairy Dust 43
Fairy Tales, The 44
Falcon's Malteser, The 57
Family From One End Street, The 67
Famous Five Series, The 60
Farmer, Penelope 66
Farmyard Tales 7
Fighting Fantasy Series 87
Finding the Fox 53
Fine, Anne 58

Finn, Rebecca 5
First Colours 9
First Cookbook 89
First Fairytales Series 6
First Nature Book 95
First Picture ABC 9
First Thousand Words Series 93
Five Go to Mystery Moor and Five on Kirrin Island Again 33
Flanagan, John 55
Flash Flood 73
Flat Stanley 41
Fletcher, Charlie 55
Flip-Flap Body Book ...96
Flour Babies 58
Football: The Ultimate Guide 90
Foreman, Michael ..15, 44
Frank, Anne 99
Freedman, Claire 20
Freedman, Dan 67
French, Fiona 23
French, Jackie 23
French, Vivian 43
Full, Full, Full of Love 23
Fun With Series 103
Funke, Cornelia 54

G

Gaiman, Neil 84
Gallop! 47
Garbage King, The 70
Gardner, Sally 15, 33, 37, 65
Garfield, Leon 44
Garnett, Eve 67
Gavin, Jamila 37
Gee, Robyn 96
George's Secret Key to the Universe 66
Gideon the Cutpurse ..66
Gift, The 77
Giraffes Can't Dance ...20
Girl, Missing 73
Girling, Brough 32
Girls in Love 68
Girls' Book, The 87
GL Learning 11+ Practise Papers 110
Gliori, Debi 15
Global Garden, The 94
Glow in the Dark Book of Space, The 96

Godbersen, Anna 80
Golding, Julia 65
Goldman, William 84
Goodnight Mister Tom 64
Goodnight Moon 8
Goosebumps Series 51
Goscinny, Rene 50
Goudge, Elizabeth 61
Grahame, Kenneth 46
Grandad's Dinosaur ..32
Grandpa Chatterji 37
Gravett, Emily 22
Gray, Kes 40
Great and Terrible Beauty, A 78
Great Elephant Chase, The 62
Greek Myths 44
Gregg, Stacy 62
Grindley, Sally 70
Grogan, John 62
Grow It, Eat It 89
Growing Up 96
Gruffalo, The 19
Guess How Much I Love You 17

H

Hairy Maclary From Donaldson's Dairy 20
Halberstam, Gaby 73
Handa's Surprise 17
Handford, Martin 87
Handwriting Today Series 105
Hanson, Paul 7
Happy Families 32
Hargreaves, Roger 13
Harris, M.G. 70
Harris, Nicholas 96
Harris, Peter 21
Harry and the Bucketful of Dinosaurs 23
Harry Potter Series 52
Hastings, Selina 101
Hatchet 60
Hawking, Lucy & Stephen 66
Hearn, Lian 77
Hergé 50
Hiaasen, Carl 62
Hibbert, Clare 90
Higgins, Chris 69
Higson, Charlie 72

Hill, Eric 11
Hill, Stuart 77
His Dark Materials Series 75
Hitler's Canary 64
Hobbit, The 76
Hoffman, Mary 25, 74
Holes 81
Holm, Anne 64
Hooper, Mary 74
Hoot 62
Horne, Richard 87
Horowitz, Anthony 57, 72, 79
Horrible Histories Series 100
Horrid Henry 38
Horse and Pony Factfile 90
How I Live Now 84
How to Be a Knight 99
How to Train Your Dragon 51
Howard, Paul 23, 26
Hubbard, Kate 64
Hucklesby, Jill 69
Hughes, Shirley 25
Hundred and One Dalmatians, The 61
Hunt, Elizabeth Singer 37
Hunter, Norman 57
Hutchins, Pat 17
Hutchinson Illustrated Treasury of Children's Literature, The 47
Hutchinson Treasury of Children's Poetry, The 45

I
I am David 64
I Can Learn Series 104
I Was a Rat 75
I, Coriander 65
Ibbotson, Eva 70, 74
in the Night Garden 10
Incredible Adventures of Professor Branestawm, The 57
Indian in the Cupboard, The 56
Ingo 77
Inkheart 54
Inkpen, Mick 10, 101
Invisible City 70
Invisible Friend, The 58
Isserlis, Steven 90

J
Jack Stalwart Series 37
Jackson, Steve 87
Jake Cake: Werewolf Teacher 39
Jamil's Clever Cat 23
Jay, Alison 101
Jeffers, Oliver 18
Jensen, Marie-Louise 74
Jeram, Anita 17
Jimmy Coates: Killer 73
John, Lauren St 61
Jolley, Mike 4
Jolly Phonics Series 28
Jolly Postman, The 22
Jones, Diana Wynne 54
Journey to the River Sea 70
Junk 82
Just Listen 83
Just William 57

K
Katie Meets the Impressionists 89
Keeper 81
Kensuke's Kingdom 63
Kerr, Judith 24, 25
Kessler, Liz 43
Kick Off, The 67
Killer Underpants, The 57
King of the Cloud Forests 63
King, Clive 58
Kingfisher History Encyclopedia, The 98
King-Smith, Dick 36
Kinney, Jeff 51
Kipper 10
Kiss That Missed, The 21
Kite Rider, The 70
Klutz 88
Knudsen, Michelle 24
Kubler, Annie 4

L
Lacey, Minna 95
Lady Grace Mysteries: a Is For Assassin 65
Ladybird Key Words Flash Cards 29
Ladybird Key Words Series 28
Ladybird Read It Yourself Series 31

Laffon, Martine 91
Laird, Elizabeth 70
Landy, Derek 54
Langrish, Katherine 55
Laura's Star and the Sleepover 32
Lawrence, Caroline 65
Lawrence, Michael 57
Legend of Spud Murphy, The 37
Let's Get Lost 83
Letts Magical Topics Series 106
Letts Revise Series 107
Letts SATS Papers 108
Letts Success SATS Series 104, 106
Lewin, Betsy 25
Lewis, CS 55
Library Lion 24
Life As We Knew It 82
Life Like Mine, A 94
Lighthouse Keeper's Lunch, The 26
Lindgren, Astrid 46
Lion, the Witch and the Wardrobe, The 55
Litchfield, Jo 9
Little Ballerina Dancing 7
Little House on the Prairie 65
Little Prince, The 41
Little White Horse 61
Little Women 46
Livingstone, Ian 87
Lloyd, Sam 8
Lodge, Jo 5
Lofting, Hugh 61
London Eye Mystery, The 67
Looking After Your Pet Series 90
Looking At Religion Series 101
Lost and Found 18
Luxe, The 80

M
Macdonald, Alan 39
Machine Gunners, The 64
MacKinnon, Catherine 4
Magic Faraway Tree, The 41
Magic Kitten Series 35

Magic Treehouse Series 41
Magorian, Michelle 64
Magyk 53
Maizels, Jennie 94
Malam, John 98
Malley, Gemma 81
Malory Towers Series 58
Manning, Sarra 83
Marley 62
Martyn Pig 73
Maths Dictionary 111
Matilda 59
Maximum Ride: The Angel Experiment 76
Mayhew, James 89
Mayo, Margaret 17
McBratney, Sam 17
McCaughrean, Geraldine 70
McEwen, Katharine 32
McKay, Hilary 67
McKee, David 18, 25
McKenzie, Sophie 73
Meadows, Daisy 42
Mediator Series 78
Meerkat Mail 22
Meg and Mog 17
Melling, David 21, 40
Meredith, Sue 94, 96, 101
Meyer, Stephenie 78
Michael Foreman's Nursery Rhymes 15
Midnight For Charlie Bone 53
Millard, Anne 98
Milligan, Spike 45
Milly-Molly-Mandy Storybook, The 36
Milne, A.A. 12
Minis Series 6
Miskin, Ruth 27, 28
Mister Magnolia 18
Mister Monday 55
Mitton, Tony 24
Mixed Up Fairy Tales 22
Mog the Forgetful Cat 25
Monks, Lydia 20
Monsterology 47
Moore, Inga 24
Morpurgo, Michael 44, 63
Mortal Engines 77
Mr Men 13
Mrs Pepperpot Stories 41

Muchamore, Robert 72
Muddle Farm 22
Mugford, Simon 97
Murphy, Glenn 91
Murphy, Jill 21, 41
Mustard, Custard,
Grumble Belly and
Gravy 45
My Big Science Book ..97
My Brother's Famous
Bottom 40
My Fairy Princess
Palace 22
My Favourite Nursery
Rhymes 15
My First Signs 4
My Mummy's Bag 7
My Naughty Little
Sister 39
My So-Called Life 80
My Story Series 100
My Swordhand
is Singing 79
My Terrific Tractor Book.7
Mystic and the
Midnight Ride 62

N

Nabb, Magdalen 43
Nadin, Joanna 80
Naughtiest Girl in
the School, The 58
Nelly the Monster
Sitter 40
Newes from the
Dead 74
Nicholls, Sally 67
Nicoll, Helen 17
Night Pirates, The 21
Nimmo, Jenny 53
Nix, Garth 55, 76
Noisy Noisy Series 6
Nolan, Tina 35
Noon, Steve 98
North Child 77
Northern Lights 75
Norton, Mary 56
Not Now Bernard 18
Noughts and Crosses .82
Nursery Rhymes 15

O

Old MacDonald
Puppet Book 5
One Snowy Night 21

Orchard Book of Aesop's
Fables, The 44
Osborne, Mary Pope 41
Ottoline and the
Yellow Cat 36
Owl Babies 21
Owl Who Was Afraid
of the Dark, The 26
Oxenbury, Helen 20
Oxford Dictionaries 92
Oxford Illustrated
Encyclopedia 92
Oxford Reading
Tree Read At
Home Flashcards
Wordgames 29
Oxford Reading Tree
Read At Home Series.. 29
Oxford School French
Dictionary 93

P

Paddington 13
Pants Ahoy! 51
Paolini, Christopher 76
Parker-Rees, Guy ...20, 24
Parsons, Jayne 95
Patterson, James 76
Pattou, Edith 77
Paul, Korky 24
Paulsen, Gary 60
Paver, Michelle 61
Peace At Last 21
Pearce, Philippa 66
Peet, Mal 81, 83
Penderwicks, The 67
Penguin 18
Percy Jackson and
the Lightning Thief 53
Periodic Table, The 111
Peter Rabbit 13
Petty, Kate 94
Pfeffer, Susan 82
Pfister, Marcus 26
Philip's Modern
School Atlas 93
Philips, Mike 87
Picture Atlas 93
Pienkowski, Jan 17, 44
Pilkey, Dav 51
Pippi Longstocking 46
Pirate School: Just a
Bit of Wind 32
Pirateology 47
Playtime Peekaboo 4
Playtime Rhymes 15

Please Mrs Butler 45
Poskitt, Kjartan 57
Possessing Rayne 78
Potter, Beatrix 13
Pratchett, Terry 76
Princess Bride, The 84
Princess Diaries, The ..80
Private Peaceful 63
Proysen, Alf 41
Puffin Book of Fantastic
First Poems, The 45
Pullman, Philip 75

R

Rai, Bali 82
Rainbow Fish, The 26
Rainbow Fun 4
Rainbow Magic
Series 42
Ranger's Apprentice:
The Ruins of Gorlan,
The 55
Ransford, Sandy 90
Ransome, Arthur 60
Raven's Gate 79
Read Write Inc Series .28
Readman, Jo 94
Real Fairy Storybook,
The 33
Recruit, The 72
Rees, Celia 74
Rees, Gwyneth 43
Reeve, Philip 57, 77
Remembrance 74
Rennison, Louise 80
Resistance 73
Revolting Rhymes 45
Reynolds, Adrian 18, 23
Richardson, E.E. 79
Riddell, Chris 36
Rinaldo, Luana 4
Riordan, Rick 53
Roald Dahl Treasury,
The 47
Roberts, David 39
Roberts, Ley Honor 94
Robinson, Hilary 22
Robinson, Tony 98
Robson, Peter 111
Rock, Lois 101
Rodgers, Frank 32
Roman Mysteries
Series, The 65
Room on the Broom 19

Rosen, Michael 20, 45
Rosie's Walk 17
Rosoff, Meg 84
Ross, Tony 15
Rowling, J.K. 52
RSPB My First Book
of Garden Birds 95
Rubies in the Snow 64
Ruby in the Smoke 75
Rusbridger, Alan 35
Russell the Sheep 21
Ryan, Chris 73

S

Sabriel 76
Sabuda, Robert 46
Sachar, Louis 81
Saffy's Angel 67
Sage, Alison 45, 47
Sage, Angie 53
Said, S.F. 61
Saint-Exupery,
Antoine De 41
Sam the Stolen
Puppy 35
Say Hello to the
Animals 8
Scarlett 69
Scarry, Richard 26
Scheffler, Axel 19, 22
Schonell, Fred J 105
Scotton, Rob 21
Secret Countess, The ..74
Secret Diary of Adrian
Mole Aged 13 ¾, The ...80
Seder, Rufus Butler 47
Sedgwick, Marcus 79
See How It's Made 97
See Inside Ancient
Rome 99
See Inside Planet
Earth 94
Seeing Stone, The 65
Selfish Crocodile, The 23
Sendak, Maurice 18
Series of Unfortunate
Events, A 57
Serraillier, Ian 64
Seuss, Dr. 12
Shakespeare Stories ...44
Shan, Darren 79
Sharratt, Nick 22, 44
Shiraz: The Ibiza
Diaries 80

Silver Sword, The **64**

Silverfin **72**

Simon, Francesca **38**

Simpson, Craig **73**

Sir Charlie Stinkysocks
and the Really Big
Adventure **25**

Six Dinner Sid **24**

Skellig **81**

Skelton, Matthew **54**

Skin **59**

Skulduggery Pleasant **54**

Smith, Alistair **96**

Smith, Dodie **61**

Snail and the Whale,
The **19**

Snicket, Lemony **57**

Snow, Alan **51**

Snowman, The **22**

Snuggletime Series **4**

Sophie's Adventures **36**

Sparkes, Ali **53**

Spiderwick
Chronicles, The **56**

Spilled Water **70**

Spinelli, Jerry **81**

Splish, Splash, Splosh **5**

Spook's Apprentice,
The **54**

Spot **10**

Spud Goes Green **94**

Spy Dog **40**

Stanton, Andy **39**

Stargirl **81**

Starting Chess **90**

Steer, Dugald **47**

Stephenson, Kristina **25**

Stern, Sam **89**

Stevenson,
Robert Louis **46**

Stig of the Dump **58**

Stine, R.L. **51**

Stone Goblins **40**

Stoneheart **55**

Stories Jesus Told **101**

Stormbreaker **72**

Storr, Catherine **36**

Story of Tracy
Beaker, The **68**

Stravaganza:
City of Masks **74**

Streatfeild, Noel **69**

Street Through
Time, A **98**

Strong, Jeremy **32, 40**

Stroud, Jonathan **54**

Subtle Knife **75**

Suitcase Kid, The **68**

Swallows and
Amazons **60**

Szirtes, Helen **87**

T

Tail of Emily
Windsnap, The **43**

Tale of Despereaux, The **56**

Tamar **83**

Tarbett, Debbie **9**

Tatchell, Judy **97**

Ten Wriggly Wiggly
Caterpillars **9**

Terry, Michael **23**

That's Not My Series **5**

Thaxton, Giles **94**

There Was An Old Lady
Who Swallowed a Fly ..**20**

There's a House Inside
My Mummy **96**

Things I Know
About Love **83**

Thomas the Tank
Engine **11**

Thomas, Valerie **24**

Three Little Pigs and
Other Stories **44**

Tiara Club Series, The **.43**

Tickle, Jack **24**

Ticktock Essential
History Guides **99**

Tiger Who Came to
Tea, The **24**

Tintin **50**

Titanic 2020 ....**60**

Tithe **78**

Toksvig, Sandi **64**

Tolkien, J.R.R. **76**

Tom's Midnight
Garden **66**

Tomlinson, Jill **26**

Topsy and Tim **9**

Townsend, Sue **80**

Treasure IsLand **46**

Troll Fell **55**

Tucker, Stephen **44**

Tumtum and Nutmeg ..**35**

Twilight **78**

Twits, The **59**

U

Uderzo, Albert **50**

(Un)Arranged
Marriage **82**

Unwin, Mike **95**

Urgum the Axeman **57**

Usborne Beginners
Series **91**

Usborne First
Experiences **9**

Usborne History of
Britain, The **99**

Usborne Internet-Linked
Encyclopedia of World
Religions **101**

Usborne Internet-Linked
Science Encyclopedia,
The **97**

Usborne Nature Trail
Series **95**

Usborne Spotters
Guides **95**

Usborne Young Reading
Scheme **31**

Utterly Me, Clarice
Bean **36**

V

Valentine, Jenny **83**

Vann, Kate Le **83**

Various, The **56**

Varjak Paw **61**

Velveteen Rabbit, The **26**

Very Busy Bee, The **24**

Very Hungry
Caterpillar, The **17**

W

Waddell, Martin **21**

Walser, David **44**

War Horse **63**

Warnes, Tim **8**

Watt, Fiona **4, 7, 88**

Ways to Live Forever **67**

We're Going on a
Bear Hunt **20**

Webb, Holly **35**

Westall, Robert **64**

Whatley, Bruce **23**

Wheels on the
Bus, The **33**

Where the Wild
Things Are **18**

Where's Wally? **87**

White Giraffe, The **61**

Whittley, Sarah **95**

Who's in the Loo? **18**

Why Beethoven
Threw the Stew **90**

Why Is Snot Green? **91**

Why Should I Bother
About the Planet? **94**

Whybrow, Ian **8, 23**

Wilder, Laura Ingalls **65**

Wilkes, Angela **89**

Williams, Marcia **44**

Williams, Margery **26**

Willis, Jeanne **18**

Wilson, Jacqueline **68**

Wind in the Willows **46**

Winnie the Pooh **12**

Winnie the Witch **24**

Winston, Robert **96**

Witch Child **74**

Witch's Dog, The **32**

Wojtowycz, David **23**

Wolf Brother **61**

Wonderful Wizard
of Oz, The **46**

World According to
Humphrey, The **35**

World Came to My
Place Today, The **94**

Worst Children's Jobs
in History, The **98**

Worst Witch, The **41**

Wow! **92**

Y

Year Full of Stories, A ...**44**

You're a Bad Man,
Mr Gum! **39**

Young Bond Series **72**

Young, Selina **44**

Z

Zephaniah, Benjamin ...**82**

Zevin, Gabrielle **81**

SUBJECT INDEX

Adoption

Girl, Missing 73
Goodnight Mister Tom **64**
Saffy's Angel 67
Story of Tracy
Beaker, The **68**

Action & Adventure
(see also spies & fantasy)

Airman **60**
A.N.T.I.D.O.T.E **60**
Diamond of Drury
Lane, The **65**
Dog Called Grk, A **62**
Family From One
End Street, The **67**
Famous Five Series **60**
Five Go to Mystery Moor
and Five on Kirrin Island
Again 33
Flash Flood 73
Gideon the Cutpurse .. **66**
Hatchet **60**
Invisible City 70
Jimmy Coates: Killer ...73
Journey to the
River Sea 70
Kensuke's Kingdom **63**
Kite Rider, The 70
Life As We Knew It **82**
Ranger's Apprentice:
The Ruins of Gorlan 55
Resistance 73
Swallows and
Amazons **60**
Tintin 50
Titanic 2020 .... **60**
Wolf Brother **61**

Alphabet

First Picture ABC 9

Animals
(see also Creepy-Crawlies,
Horses & Ponies and
Under the Sea)

All Afloat on
Noah's Boat 24
Amazing Maurice
and His Educated
Rodents, The 76
Animal Ark Series **62**
Animal Rescue Series .35

Butterfly Lion, The 63
Click, Clack, Moo:
Cows That Type 25
Coldest Day in the
Zoo, The 35
Cows in Action Series ..37
Dear Zoo 8
Diary of a Wombat 23
Doctor Dolittle Stories.. 61
Dog Called Grk, A 62
Elmer 25
Encyclopedia of
Animals 95
Enormous
Crocodile, The 26, 59
Gallop! 47
Giraffes Can't Dance ... 20
Guess How Much
I Love You 17
Hairy Maclary From
Donaldson's Dairy 20
Hundred and One
Dalmatians, The 61
Kipper 10
Library Lion 24
Little White Horse 61
Looking After Your
Pet Series 90
Magic Kitten Series 35
Marley 62
Meerkat Mail 22
Mog the
Forgetful Cat 25
One Snowy Night 21
Orchard Book of
Aesop's Fables, The 44
Peter Rabbit 13
Rosie's Walk 17
Russell the Sheep 21
Sam the Stolen
Puppy 35
Say Hello to the
Animals 8
Selfish Crocodile, The 23
Six Dinner Sid 24
Sophie's Adventures 36
Spot 11
Spy Dog 40
Tale of Despereaux,
The 56
Tiger Who Came
to Tea, The 24
Tumtum and Nutmeg ...35
Varjak Paw 61

White Giraffe, The 61
Who's in the Loo? 18
Wind in the
Willows, The 46
Witch's Dog, The 32
Wolf Brother 61
World According to
Humphrey, The 35

Ballet

Ballerina 88
Ballet Shoes 69
Ballet Treasury 90
Little Ballerina
Dancing Book 7

Bedtime

Goodnight Moon 8
Kiss That Missed, The .. 21
Laura's Star and the
Sleepover 32
Night Pirates, The 21
One Snowy Night 21
Owl Babies 21
Owl Who Was Afraid
of the Dark, The 26
Peace At Last 21
Russell the Sheep 21
Where the Wild
Things Are 18

Bullying

Boy With Lightning
Feet, The 37
Chocolate War, The 82
Hoot 62
Invisible Friend, The 58
Matilda 59
Stargirl 81

Counting

Catch That Goat! 9
Handa's Surprise 17
Mister Magnolia 18
Ten Wriggly, Wiggly
Caterpillars 9
Very Hungry
Caterpillar, The 17

Creepy-Crawlies

Aaaarrgghh, Spider! 20
Bug Hunter 95

Clackety Clacks: Bee 4
Very Busy Bee, The 24
Very Hungry
Caterpillar, The 17

Death

Before I Die 84
Broken Soup 83
Deeper Than Blue 69
Elsewhere 81
Let's Get Lost 83
Martyn Pig 73
Newes From the
Dead 74
Sabriel 76
Ways to Live Forever ...67

Dinosaurs

Astrosaurs Series 40
Dinosaur Atlas 98
Dinosaurs 98
Grandad's Dinosaur 32
Harry and the Bucketful
of Dinosaurs 23

Divorce &
Family Breakdown

Broken Soup 83
Scarlett 69
Suitcase Kid, The 68

Dragons

Dragonology 47
Eragon 76
Hobbit, The 76
How to Train Your
Dragon 51

Eating Disorders

Girls in Love 68
How I Live Now 84
Just Listen 83

Environment &
Conservation

Hoot 62
Keeper 81
Life As We Knew It 82
See Inside Planet
Earth 94
Spud Goes Green 94

Why Should I Bother About the Planet? 94

Faeries & Fairies

Artemis Fowl 56
Artemis Fowl: The Graphic Novel 51
Fairy Dust 43
I, Coriander 65
My Fairy Princess Palace 22
Rainbow Magic Series 42
Real Fairy Storybook 33
Spiderwick Chronicles, The 56
Tithe 78
Various, The 56

Fairytales

Three Little Pigs and Other Stories 44
Fairy Tales, The 44
First Fairytales Series 6
Jolly Postman, The 22
Ladybird Read it Yourself 31
Mixed Up Fairy Tales 22
Revolting Rhymes 45

Family

Ballet Shoes 69
Breadwinner, The 70
Broken Soup 83
Charlie and Lola 12
Children Who Smelled a Rat, The 32
Cosmic 66
Dogger 25
Family From One End Street, The 67
Full, Full, Full of Love 23
Grandpa Chatterji 37
Happy Families 32
Little House on the Prairie 65
Little Women 46
Milly-Molly-Mandy Storybook, The 36
My Brother's Famous Bottom 40
My Naughty Little Sister 39
Penderwicks, The 67
Saffy's Angel 67

Spilled Water 70
Urgum the Axeman 57
We're Going on a Bear Hunt 20

Fantasy

Across the Nightingale Floor 77
Amazing Maurice and His Educated Rodents, The 76
Amulet of Samarkand, The 54
Artemis Fowl 56
Artemis Fowl: The Graphic Novel 51
Beast Quest Series 37
Belgariad: Pawn of Prophecy, The 84
Borrowers, The 56
Charmed Life 54
City of Ember, The 55
Cry of the Icemark, The 77
Dark Is Rising Sequence, The 76
Endymion Spring 54
Eragon 76
Fighting Fantasy Series 87
Finding the Fox 53
Gift, The 77
Great and Terrible Beauty, A 78
Harry Potter Series 52
His Dark Materials Series 75
Hobbit, The 76
Indian in the Cupboard, The 56
Ingo 77
Inkheart 54
Lion, the Witch and the Wardrobe, The 55
Little Prince, The 41
Magic Faraway Tree, The 41
Magic Treehouse Series 41
Magyk 53
Maximum Ride: The Angel Experiment 76
Midnight For Charlie Bone 53
Mister Monday 55
Mortal Engines 77
Mrs Pepperpot Stories 41

North Child 77
Percy Jackson and the Lightning Thief 53
Princess Bride, The 84
Sabriel 76
Skulduggery Pleasant 54
Spiderwick Chronicles, The 56
Spook's Apprentice, The 54
Stoneheart 55
Stravaganza: City of Masks 74
Troll Fell 55
Various, The 56
Wonderful Wizard of Oz, The 46

Farm

Click, Clack, Moo: Cows That Type 25
Farm 5
Farmyard Tales 7
Muddle Farm 22
My Terrific Tractor Book 7
Old Macdonald Puppet Book 5
Rosie's Walk 17
Say Hello to the Animals 8

Fear & Worries

Dogger 25
Laura's Star and the Sleepover 32
Owl Babies 21
Owl Who Was Afraid of the Dark, The 26

Football

Boy With the Lightning Feet, The 37
Football: The Ultimate Guide 90
Keeper 81
Kick Off, The 67

Friendship

BFG, The 59
Boy in the Striped Pyjamas, The 84
Deeper Than Blue 69
Invisible Friend, The 58
Lost and Found 18
Penguin 18

Rainbow Fish, The 26
Selfish Crocodile, The 23
Snail and the Whale, The 19
Snowman, The 22
Stig of the Dump 58
Tom's Midnight Garden 66

Funny

1001 Really Stupid Jokes 87
Adventures of Captain Underpants, The 51
Aliens Love Underpants 20
Angus, Thongs and Full-Frontal Snogging 80
Arabel's Raven 40
Artemis Fowl 56
Artemis Fowl: The Graphic Novel 51
Asterix 50
Astrosaurs Series 40
Calm Down Boris 8
Child's Treasury of Milligan, A 48
Cows in Action Series 37
Diary of a Wimpy Kid 51
Diary of a Wombat 23
Dirty Bertie: Burp! 39
Falcon's Malteser, The 57
Horrid Henry 38
How to Train Your Dragon 51
Incredible Adventures of Professor Branestawm, The 57
Jake Cake: Werewolf Teacher 39
Just William 57
Killer Underpants, The 57
Mustard, Custard, Grumble Belly and Gravy 45
My Brother's Famous Bottom 40
My So-Called Life 80
Nelly the Monster Sitter 40
Not Now Bernard 18
Pants Ahoy! 51
Pippi Longstocking 46
Princess Bride, The 84
Princess Diaries, The 80
Revolting Rhymes 45
Roald Dahl 59

Secret Diary of Adrian
Mole Aged 13 ¾ 80
Series of Unfortunate
Events, A 57
Shiraz: Ibiza Diaries 80
Spy Dog 40
Stone Goblins 40
Urgum the Axeman 57
Who's in the Loo? 18
You're a Bad Man,
Mr Gum! 39

Ghosts

Goosebumps Series 51
Invisible Friend, The 58
Mediator Series, The 78

History

Danger Zone Series 99
Horrible Histories 100
Kingfisher History
Encyclopedia, The 98
Street Through
Time, A 98
Ticktock Essential
History Guides 99
Usborne History of
Britain, The 99
Worst Children's Jobs
in History 98

History: Prehistoric

Stig of the Dump 58
Wolf Brother 61

History: Egyptians

Egyptology 47

History: Greeks

Greek Myths 44
Percy Jackson and the
Lightning Thief 53

History: Romans

Asterix 50
Roman Mysteries
Series 65
See Inside Ancient
Rome 99

History: Vikings

How to Train Your
Dragon 51
Troll Fell 55

History: Middle Ages

Seeing Stone, The 65

History: Tudors

Lady Grace Mysteries:
a Is For Assassin 65

History: 17th Century

I, Coriander 65
Newes From the
Dead 74
Witch Child 74

History: 18th Century

Diamond of Drury Lane,
The 65
Gideon the Cutpurse ...66

History: 19th Century

Little House on
the Prairie 65
Luxe, The 80

History: Victorians

Between Two Seas 74
Great and Terrible
Beauty, A 78
Ruby in the Smoke 75
Tom's Midnight
Garden 66

History:
Early 20th Century

Secret Countess, The ...74

History:
First World War

Charlotte Sometimes ...66
Private Peaceful 63
Remembrance 74
Rubies in the Snow 64
War Horse 63

History:
Second World War

Boy in the Striped
Pyjamas, The 84
Diary of a Young Girl,
The 99
Goodnight Mister Tom 64
Hitler's Canary 64
I am David 64
King of the Cloud
Forests 63

Machine Gunners,
The 64
Resistance 73
Silver Sword, The 64
Tamar 83

Horror &
Scary Stories

Cirque Du Freak 79
Coraline 84
Darkside 79
Demonata Series 79
Devil's Footsteps, The ...79
Goosebumps Series 51
My Swordhand Is
Singing 79
Raven's Gate 79
Spook's Apprentice,
The 54
Twilight 78

Horses & Ponies

Enchanted Horse, The 43
Horse and Pony
Factfile 90
Mystic and the
Midnight Rider 62
War Horse 63

Illness or Disability

32C That's Me
(breast cancer) 69
Broken Soup
(depression) 83
Deeper Than Blue
(loss of limb) 69
Face
(facial disfiguration) 82
London Eye Mystery,
The (asperger's
syndrome).......................67
Saffy's Angel
(wheelchair)...................67
Skellig (baby with
heart problems) 81
Stravaganza: City of
Masks (cancer) 74
Things I Know About
Love (leukaemia) 83
Velveteen Rabbit, The
(scarlet fever) 26
Ways to Live Forever
(leukaemia) 67

Jungle

Giraffes Can't Dance ...20
Journey to the

River Sea 70
Selfish Crocodile, The . 23

Knights & Castles

How to Be a Knight 99
Kiss That Missed, The ..21
Ranger's Apprentice:
The Ruins of Gorlan 55
Seeing Stone, The 65
Sir Charlie Stinkysocks
and the Really Big
Adventure 25

Love & Romance

Angus, Thongs and
Full-Frontal Snogging .. 80
Blue Sky Freedom 73
Between Two Seas 74
Broken Soup 83
Girls in Love 68
Guess How Much
I Love You 17
Full, Full, Full of Love .. 23
How I Live Now 84
Just Listen 83
Let's Get Lost 83
Luxe, The 80
Mediator Series, The 78
North Child 77
Noughts and Crosses .82
Princess Diaries, The ...80
Secret Countess, The ..74
Tamar 83
Things I Know
About Love 83
Twilight 78
Velveteen Rabbit, The 26

Multicultural

Amazing Grace 25
Blue Sky Freedom 73
Breadwinner, The 70
Catch That Goat! 9
Christophe's Story 36
Does My Head Look
Big in This? 83
Face 82
Full, Full, Full of Love .. 23
Garbage King, The 70
Grandpa Chatterji 37
Handa's Surprise 17
Jamil's Clever Cat 23
Life Like Mine, A 94
Noughts and Crosses .82

Spilled Water 70

(Un)arranged
Marriage 82

Mysteries

Falcon's Malteser, the ..57

Famous Five Series 60

Five Go to Mystery
Moor and Five on
Kirrin Island Again 33

Lady Grace Mysteries:
A Is For Assassin 65

London Eye
Mystery, The 67

Ottoline and the
Yellow Cat 36

Roman Mysteries
Series 65

Ruby in the Smoke 75

Pirates

Night Pirates, The 21

Pirate School: Just
a Bit of Wind 32

Pirateology 47

Treasure Island 46

Princesses

My Fairy Princess
Palace 22

Princess Bride, The 84

Princess Diaries, The ..80

Tiara Club Series 43

Racism

Blue Sky Freedom 73

Face 82

Noughts and Crosses ..82

School

Adventures of Captain
Underpants, The 51

Charlotte Sometimes .. 66

Children Who Smelled
a Rat, The 32

Chocolate War, The 82

Demon Headmaster,
The 58

Diary of a Wimpy Kid 51

Finding the Fox 53

Flour Babies 58

Great and Terrible
Beauty, A 78

Harry Potter Series 52

Invisible Friend, The 58

Malory Towers Series ...58

Naughtiest Girl in the
School, The 58

Please Mrs Butler 45

Stargirl 81

Tiara Club Series 43

World According to
Humphrey, The 35

Worst Witch, The 41

Science & Maths
(see also Space)

Body 96

Dorling Kindersley
Celebrity Science
Series 97

Flip-Flap Body Book ... 96

My Big Science Book ...97

Number Devil, The 66

See How It's Made 97

Usborne Internet-Linked
Science Encyclopedia,
The 97

Seaside

Laura's Star and
the Sleepover 32

Lighthouse Keeper's
Lunch, The 26

Self Confidence

Amazing Grace 25

Elmer 25

Giraffes Can't Dance ...20

Stargirl 81

Space

Aliens Love
Underpants 20

Astrosaurs Series 40

Cosmic 66

Doctor Who 50

George's Secret Key
to the Universe 66

Glow in the Dark Book
of Space, The 96

Spies

Alex Rider Series 72

Cherub Series 72

Jack Stalwart Series 37

Spy Dog 40

Young Bond Series 72

Transport

Big Busy Book of
Richard Scarry, The 26

Thomas the Tank
Engine 11

Trucks & Diggers

Dig, Dig Digging 17

My Terrific Tractor Book 7

Under the Sea

Commotion in the
Ocean 23

Ingo 77

Snail and the Whale,
The 19

Tail of Emily
Windsnap, The 43

Rainbow Fish, The 26

War
(see also History)

How I Live Now 84

Witches & Wizards

Amulet of Samarkand,
The 54

Charmed Life 54

Harry Potter Series 52

Lion, the Witch and the
Wardrobe, The 55

Magyk 53

Meg and Mog 17

Room on the Broom 19

Skulduggery Pleasant 54

Winnie the Witch 24

Witch Child 74

Witch's Dog, The 32

Wonderful Wizard of
Oz, The 46

Worst Witch, The 41

Zoo

Coldest Day in the
Zoo, the 35

Dear Zoo 8